ROYAL COMMISSION ON HISTC
SUPPLEMENTARY SERIES: 1

R. S. Fitzgerald

Liverpool Road Station, Manchester

An historical and architectural survey

MANCHESTER UNIVERSITY PRESS

in association with the
Royal Commission on Historical Monuments

and the
Greater Manchester Council

Published by

Manchester University Press
Oxford Road, Manchester M13 9PL

in association with the
Royal Commission on Historical Monuments
(England)
and the
Greater Manchester Council

British Library cataloguing-in-publication data

Fitzgerald, R. S.
Liverpool Road Station, Manchester.
1. Manchester, Eng. Liverpool Road Station.
I. Title. II. Royal Commission on Historical Monuments
(England).
385'.314   TF302.M/

ISBN 0 7190 0790 9   paperback
     0 7190 0765 8   hard covers

Printed in Great Britain

by
Elliott Brothers & Yeoman Ltd
Speke, Liverpool L24 9JL

Contents

Foreword

When the Liverpool and Manchester Railway was opened in 1830 neither the Royal Commission on Historical Monuments nor the Greater Manchester Council was in existence; but both of them are in a sense its creations. The changes in all aspects of life in England which the Railway heralded brought about the vast conurbation which today is Greater Manchester and in so doing created the need for a body like the R.C.H.M. to record and study those earlier constructions which the changes were putting at risk. It is therefore fitting, now that the Railway itself has become a subject of academic study and historic conservation, that the two bodies should combine to produce the present volume. It is intended both to celebrate the 150th anniversary of the Railway and to make a contribution to the study of the archaeology and architecture of the nineteenth century.

Mr R. S. Fitzgerald, B.Sc., Keeper of the Leeds Museum of Science and Industry, was invited to undertake the task, and it is a pleasure to place on record here our gratitude to Mr P. J. Kelley, Director of the Museum, and Mr M. C. Palmer-Jones, M.A., Director of Leisure Services of the City of Leeds, for their readiness to grant him leave of absence, effectively on secondment to the Commission, for that purpose. It is an equal pleasure to thank Mr Fitzgerald himself for the vast amount of recording, research and writing that he carried out in a very short time. The Commission guided the investigation and its publication throughout but the volume is essentially Mr Fitzgerald's work. We are particularly happy that this, the first of a numbered series of Commission Occasional Publications, should be on such a subject and the result of such co-operation.

We would thank all those members of the Royal Commission on Historical Monuments, of Greater Manchester Council and Manchester University Press whose collaboration has made the book possible. We hope that it may be the first of many other volumes produced jointly by the Commission and a local government authority.

Adeane
  The Rt. Hon. the Lord Adeane, P.C., G.C.B., G.C.V.O.
  Chairman, Royal Commission on
  Historical Monuments (England)

P. Buckley
  County Councillor Dr Patrick Buckley
  Chairman, Greater Manchester Council

Acknowledgements

The author wishes to express his gratitude to the following for their assistance in the compilation of this book. John Morrey, of the Royal Commission on Historical Monuments; Ken Powell; Robert Walker; R. C. Ormiston-Chant; and Peter Langan, all of whom helped with the survey work, often in unpleasant and sometimes in dangerous situations. My special thanks are due to Mr A. Arschavir, of the School of Architecture, Manchester University, who was responsible for organising the drawings of the Merchants' Company Warehouse, and to the students who carried out the work. To the Librarians and staff of the Manchester City Library and Archives Department, the City of Liverpool Library, Paul Rees of the Liverpool City Museum, the staff of the Leeds City Library, Commercial and Technical Section, and Darlington Public Library I am indebted for their courteous attention to my often less than rational approach to their collections. Similarly to the staff of the Public Record Office my thanks are due. More generally, by allowing access to their buildings, Mr Hooson, the owner of the Pease Warehouse, Hull; Mr P. Wiles, the Industrial Development Officer of the City of Hull; Mr D. Fisher, the Property Manager of the Aire and Calder Navigation, Mr McDermott of Granada Television, and Councillor Mark Andrews of the Sowerby Bridge Marina Development, have given the section on warehouses a greater depth than would otherwise have been possible. Mr R. J. Coon, the Chief Civil Engineer, British Railways, London Midland Region, and the engineering staff at Hampstead Road, have also assisted me in various matters concerning the bridges, and again my thanks are due to them. I owe a special debt to the librarians and staff of the Institution of Civil Engineers and the Institution of Mechanical Engineers for their efforts on my behalf, as also to Bob Weston and Paul Calvocoressi of G.L.C. Historic Buildings, and to Chris Makepeace of G.M.C. Planning Department. Clive Luhrs and Alan Chorlton of the Liverpool Road Station Society saved me much time by allowing me to make free use of their already extensive research. Finally, to the Leisure Services Department and to Leeds City Museum, represented by Mr M. Palmer-Jones and Mr P. Kelley respectively, I wish to extend my thanks for arranging my sabbatical leave, without which none of this would have been possible, and to Mrs P. Dwyer, who was faced with perhaps the most difficult job of all, typing the manuscript from my execrable handwriting.

Chapter I

The surveys and Bills

I was not long in the witness box before I began to wish for a hole to creep out at. [George Stephenson, after his examination by the parliamentary committee in 1825 on the first Liverpool and Manchester Railway Bill]

By September 1980 the Liverpool and Manchester Railway will have been in continuous operation for 150 years. Its pioneering status has on occasion been a subject of contention, but the fact remains that from its inception the line was viewed as a momentous achievement in transport history. For this reason it has not lacked historians. Most recently R. E. Carlson's *Liverpool & Manchester Railway Project* has given a detailed account of the events leading up to the public opening in September 1830. For the purpose of the present work, upon the Manchester terminus of the line, only a brief account is necessary of the general course of events prior to that date.

The earliest detailed survey for a railway between Liverpool and Manchester was undertaken in 1821 by William James, an indefatigable promoter of railways, and a supporter of George Stephenson. Although the fieldwork for the survey was completed, James failed to produce, or at least the Railway Company did not receive, the finished plans and sections. This resulted in an early crisis for the Railway, whose intention it had been to apply to Parliament for the necessary powers during the session of 1823. James's recalcitrance and subsequent financial failure compelled the Railway Company to commission a fresh survey, which was undertaken by George Stephenson. Stephenson's previous railway enterprises had been confined to the north-eastern coalfield, but his reputation as a railway builder, and more particularly as a mechanical engineer associated with the development of rails and steam locomotives, was national.

Stephenson's survey was conducted during 1824, in the teeth of opposition from local interests and under the pressure of the need to have the plans and sections ready by the beginning of the 1825 session. The Bill was presented in February 1825, and began its second reading on 2 March. By this time, opposition to the passage of the Act had been fully mobilised, and the debate on the floor of the House was proving inconclusive. To resolve the issues, it was proposed that further conduct of the proceedings be undertaken by committee, and steps were taken accordingly. What followed was to prove singularly mortifying for both Stephenson and the Liverpool and Manchester Railway Company.

Writing in 1830, Henry Booth,[1] the secretary to the Company, ascribed the failure of the first Bill to the opposition's successful contention that the existing transport facilities were adequate, that locomotives were an unsightly nuisance, that the levels and sections were erroneous and that the estimates were unrealistic.

The success of the anti-railway interest in substantiating the first two points was probably limited,[2] but on the last two they were devastatingly successful. In the course of the cross-examination their counsel, Edward Hall Alderson, entirely demolished Stephenson's testimony about the route that the line should follow. For much of this Stephenson was himself to blame. The force of the opposition's argument was directly related to the weakness of the Railway Company's case. Adept as Alderson's cross-examination was, he achieved little when confronted with sound evidence.[3] Rastrick and Wood, the two other engineering witnesses called by the Company, were unmoved by him, indeed at one point Rastrick raised some amusement at Alderson's expense over the question of the adhesive effort available in locomotives. Equally, Alderson's examination of Stephenson on locomotives was frustrated, for in that area, where his knowledge was most intimate, Stephenson was adequate to the occasion. When the cross-examination turned to the plans and sections, however, Stephenson's case crumbled. Not only were the levels proved to be incorrect but his ideas about the way the major civil engineering features were to be executed were exposed as rudimentary.

The conditions under which the survey was carried out have now become part of railway folklore and possibly they played a part in the resulting fiasco, but, as Francis Giles, a witness for the opposition, was to point out, surveys had been successfully executed under similar circumstances.[4] In the main the fault lay in Stephenson's attitude towards this aspect of the work. There is sufficient evidence to show that he exercised only the most cursory supervision over the execution of the survey. Writing to Thomas Longridge of the Bedlington Ironworks,[5] Stephenson said, '. . . The Liverpool line will soon be finished. I have Hugh [Steel] and Mr Galloway carrying on the levels who will manage the whole line without any assistance. They have now got nearly half way and through the worst of it . . .' Further substance is given to the impression that he played little part in the fieldwork by Smiles's statement[6] with reference to the Stockton and Darlington Railway '. . . that at no subsequent time did Mr. Stephenson take the sights through the spirit level with his own hands and eyes as he did on this railway . . .'.

Commenting on the collapse of the Bill, Robert Stephenson wrote to Longridge from South America.[7] '. . . It is to be regretted that my father placed the conducting of the levelling under the care of young men without experience. Simple as the process of levelling may appear, it is one of those things that requires care and dexterity in its performance . . .' As Robert had perceived, the real fault was not so much that the survey had been delegated, but rather that his father had entrusted it to two wholly inexperienced assistants.

In his biography of the Stephensons, Rolt[8] drew attention to the firm of George Stephenson & Co., which was established in an attempt to secure a monopoly of railway construction in Britain. With George and Robert Stephenson as joint chief engineers, the country was to be divided into regions served by respective trunk routes. The construction of these lines was to be delegated to a number of junior assistants: the London and Northern road was to be the domain of Joseph Locke, Robert Taylor and Elijah Galloway as chief assistants to Robert Stephenson; the London and South Wales road was to go to Hugh Steel, Thomas Gooch and Paul Padley, whilst the Liverpool and Manchester line was to be under Thomas Storey.

With the exception of Hugh Steel all were to proceed to distinguished railway careers, but at the time of the inauguration of the Company their collective experience in civil engineering was severely limited.

Not until 1825 did Locke undertake his first essay in railway construction with the short Black Fell Colliery Railway to the Tyne.[9] In the same year Thomas Gooch, with Locke, carried out survey work for the Newcastle and Carlisle Railway, his first work in railway construction.[10] Both had previously been exclusively engaged in mechanical engineering at the Forth Street Works. Storey and Padley were rather more experienced. Padley[11] was a qualified surveyor and the brother-in-law of William James, to whom he had acted as principal assistant on the first Liverpool and Manchester Railway survey. Thomas Storey[12] was by training a colliery viewer, but was eventually to occupy a prominent position as engineer and traffic manager of the Stockton and Darlington Railway; this, however, after 1825.

Although the firm of George Stephenson & Co. failed, it was from there that the talent for the construction of the Liverpool and Manchester Railway was drawn, and thence came Steel and Galloway to bear the burden of the 1825 survey. Of Steel virtually nothing is now known apart from the fact that he was a board apprentice to George Stephenson.[13] Elijah Galloway survived the events of 1825 to become established as a mechanical engineer.[14]

Central to the case for the opposition was the evidence of Francis Giles. Giles's unfortunate comments upon the practicability of crossing Chat Moss have tended to obscure the fact that in selecting him to examine Stephenson's work the opposition were employing one of the most highly respected surveyors of the day. His career began as a land surveyor with his brother, Netlam Giles.[15] In 1803 he joined John Rennie Snr, whom he served as a surveyor working upon canal, sea defence and harbour works. For Rennie and with Rennie's son, John, he carried out the complex survey for the new harbour facilities for the Scotland–Ireland cross-channel packet. John Rennie Jnr learned the profession from him, and in his autobiography[16] gave unstinting praise to Giles's abilities as a surveyor. Giles was, however, a surveyor rather than a civil engineer, and the criticism which eventually surrounded his testimony arose largely from his comments on civil engineering rather than surveying.

Like Stephenson before him, Giles delegated his survey to an assistant, but, unlike Galloway and Steel, Alexander Comrie had extensive experience of surveying. Together Giles and Comrie took the levels three times over, back-checking each time.[17] Stephenson's survey was revealed to be massively in error. The culpability of Stephenson and his assistants was the greater because the misalignments were not based upon a single mistaken level but upon a whole series of separate mistakes which had accumulated towards the Manchester termination of the line. According to Stephenson, the difference between the Vauxhall Road bench mark and Manchester Quay Street was 51 ft. 5 in., whilst Comrie found it to be 22 ft., and that between the Irwell and the Liverpool bench mark 44 ft. to Comrie's 14 ft. The Irwell itself was thus, according to Stephenson, 30 ft. above Vauxhall Road, whereas in fact it was 5 ft. below. Comrie found repeated errors all the way along the line of the survey often amounting to as much as 30 ft.

The survey by Giles and Comrie was the most complete presented by the opponents of the Bill, but the attack was pressed home by George Leather, who had himself carried out a partial survey.[18] Leather's background in engineering was rather more complete than that of Giles. Unlike Giles, moreover, he could claim previous experience in railway construction. His father had been responsible for the Fenton family's railway system connecting their collieries east of Leeds with the river Aire. George Leather had taken over from his father in the capacity of Fenton's colliery engineer, and had projected and built the extensive system of railways over the Beeston and Hunslet area of Leeds. He was also employed by Rennie as resident engineer on the Aire and Calder Navigation, in which capacity he had been responsible for several notable bridges. He had worked on Stephen-

son's home ground, surveying for a proposed canal projected in opposition to the Stockton and Darlington Railway. At the time of the Bill he was engineer to the Tees–Weardale Railway. In the south he had superintended the construction of the London and Croydon Railway, from Wandsworth to Croydon. In his own words '. . . I have been all my life an engineer, I was brought up at first amongst railways and since that I have been employed upon canals . . .'

The testimony of George Leather[19] was as damaging to Stephenson as that of Giles. He had examined the survey and had found the sections at the Liverpool end so incorrect that he could not follow the course of the line. Inspection indicated a similar state of affairs at the Manchester end. He had taken levels at the latter end only, and found that the alignment proposed by Stephenson, given the correct levels, would render the line liable to flooding. '. . . I have seen the section of a great many important works that have been undertaken by engineers and I never saw any section for a great and important work so erroneous as that which has been submitted to the committee . . .' was his final crushing comment.

Nor was the condemnation of Stephenson confined to the opposition. Prior to the parliamentary proceedings the erroneous levels had become apparent both to Stephenson and to the directors of the Railway Company. In an effort to forestall the opposition, the directors had called in William Cubitt, an established engineer whose reputation rested upon his improvements to windmills and to the treadmill. He had gone over the line with Steel and his own assistants to effect some revisions. Whatever the Company may have wished to achieve by this, its efforts were counter-productive, for Alderson seized the opportunity to force Cubitt to admit that nowhere had he found Stephenson's levels to be correct.

Disastrous in themselves, the levelling errors had important consequences. As the later canal engineers had found, expeditious route-planning involved balancing as closely as possible the quantity of earth removed from cuttings with the quantity required for embankments, for each mile of haulage pushed up costs. As Leather pointed out, beyond a certain economic limit recourse would have to be made to side cuts to obtain material for embankments, whilst spoil from cuttings would require further ground for dumping. The imbalance was greatest towards the Manchester end of the line—precisely where land values were highest. To make matters worse, serious doubts were entertained over Stephenson's proposed slope angles for cuttings and embankments, his uniform 45° being generally considered to be at the limits of stability in the most favourable circumstances.[20]

The faulty levelling badly weakened the Company's case and to some extent it may also have been responsible for the other grave defect in Stephenson's proposals. Under the Bill it was intended that the railway should cross the river Irwell about forty yards downstream from its junction with the Medlock. (See map 1.) Having bridged the Irwell, the line was to curve north-east to cross the Medlock, and after passing over Regents Road, Liverpool Road, Charles Street, John Street and Quay Street it was to terminate '. . . at or near to the westerly end of a certain place called Water Street in the Township of Manchester . . . and near to a certain bridge over the River Irwell leading to, or communicating with, the new road to Eccles . . .'.[21] The Irwell crossing was crucial to the entry into Manchester and entailed bridging the line of the Mersey and Irwell Navigation (the Old Quay Company), one of the Railway Company's leading adversaries. Here, where the Company could least afford it, Stephenson had blundered badly. Questioned by Alderson, he revealed himself to be notoriously ill informed, even to the extent of being unable give the correct width of the river. On the clearance he had allowed for shipping he vaguely suggested that 15 ft. to 20 ft. would be available, but when pressed he was forced to admit that this was a mere guess. Making good the point, Alderson then implied that the headroom was little more than 10 ft. Stephenson denied this but could offer no evidence to support his view, and in consequence the figure was repeatedly put forward by Alderson in the subsequent proceedings. Asked about tidal fluctuations, Stephenson was again forced to admit that he had carried out no investigations. Referring to the Eccles Bridge, located farther upstream, Alderson pointed out that the construction depth here was 25 ft., yet on several occasions this had proved inadequate to cope with flood tides. The bridge was situated above the point of intersection with the Medlock, a river with a reputation for tidal aberrations. To cope with the combined effects of both rivers Stephenson had proposed a bridge with an even smaller capacity. Forced eventually to concede that the construction depth of the bridge might need to be as great as 29 ft., the distraught Stephenson suggested that the solution might lie in approaching the bridge by rope-worked inclines.

Counsel's attention then shifted to the course of the line from the Irwell Bridge, along the Manchester side of the river to its termination. Apart from the crossing of the Medlock, several roads would have to be intersected. The height of the Irwell Bridge would condition the way in which this was to be achieved, and counsel made great capital from the prospect of an embankment crossing prime development land—land owned by one of the main Manchester petitioners against the Bill, Mrs Atherton. Stephenson had intended to cross the area by means of a cutting, Charles Street being carried over by a bridge. Harried over the question of headroom, he proposed that the locomotives might need to lower their chimneys to pass beneath or that inclined planes worked by horse gins might serve.[22]

The onslaught continued with Francis Giles's testimony, backed by his statement that he had seen the process of bridge-building under Rennie and that he had personally been responsible for surveying all the bridges in London for him.[23] He suggested that for an iron bridge the rise–span relationship should be of the order of 1:10, citing as an example an iron bridge of 100 ft. span, requiring a soffit 10 ft. above the spring line, the latter being at least as high as the flood line. The depth of the rib at the crown of the arch would need to be from 2 ft. 6 in. to 3 ft., reducing the rise to 7 ft. 6 in., and this he considered to be below the safe limit. An iron arch presented the most favourable case, and a masonry bridge would require even greater dimensions. These considerations would suggest a masonry bridge with a soffit 26 ft. above the flood line, bringing the level of the railroad up to 30 ft. In consequence, embankments would be necessary on both sides. The nearest source of material for the embankments was Chat Moss, six miles away. Additionally, Regents Road and Liverpool Road would have to be lowered.

On 1 June 1825 the Railway Company conceded the case to the opposition and withdrew the first Liverpool and Manchester Railway Bill. It was not disposed to admit defeat, however, and resolved to resubmit the Bill the following session, urged on by supporters within Parliament. In the interim, steps were taken to give the revised Bill a better chance against its opponents.[24] It was deemed expedient to reduce the emphasis on locomotive traction, in contrast to its open advocacy in the first Bill. The Company would not insist upon locomotive traction and, if such power were employed, it would be subject to statutory restrictions. To neutralise the opposition of the Bridgewater Canal Company, the Marquis of Stafford, heir to the Bridgewater estates, was induced to take up 1,000 shares in the Railway Company.[25]

The central weakness of the 1825 Bill remained to be dealt with. As Booth wrote,[26] '. . . on the subject of the

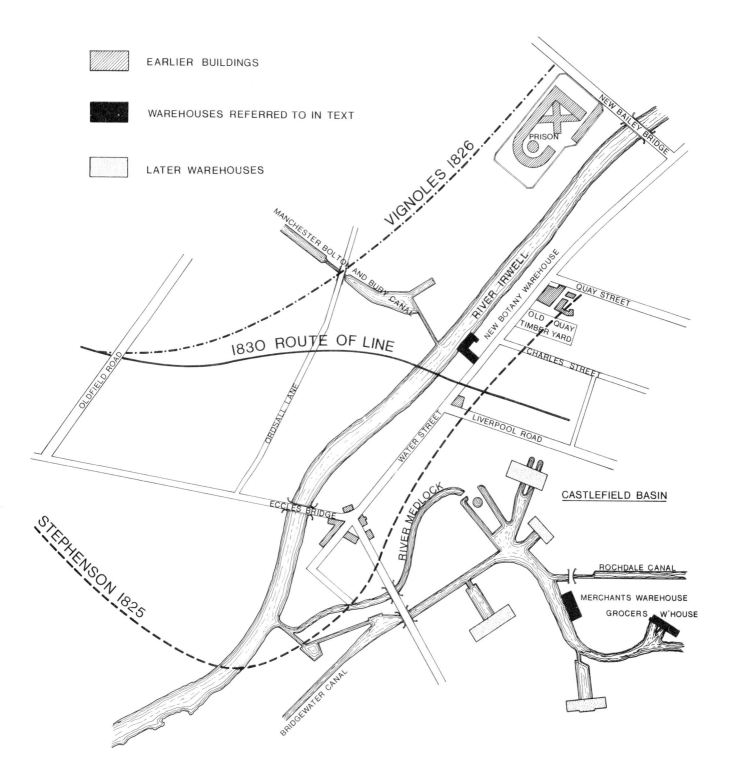

WAREHOUSES REFERRED TO IN TEXT

LATER WAREHOUSES

VIGNOLES 1826

PRISON

NEW BAILEY BRIDGE

MANCHESTER BOLTON AND BURY CANAL

RIVER IRWELL

NEW BOTANY WAREHOUSE

QUAY STREET

OLD QUAY TIMBER YARD

1830 ROUTE OF LINE

CHARLES STREET

OLDFIELD ROAD

ORDSALL LANE

WATER STREET

LIVERPOOL ROAD

ECCLES BRIDGE

RIVER MEDLOCK

CASTLEFIELD BASIN

STEPHENSON 1825

ROCHDALE CANAL

MERCHANTS WAREHOUSE

GROCERS W'HOUSE

BRIDGEWATER CANAL

Map 1. The area around the station, showing the proposed approach routes.

levels and sections, the opponents of the Bill were correct in their animadversions. A considerable error had been committed . . . and some degree of doubt and uncertainty was necessarily thrown on the whole of the surveying department.' Stephenson's reputation as a mechanical engineer remained unaffected, but his credibility as a civil engineer was entirely undermined. As later events were to prove, an important core of support remained for him on the Railway board, but the Company could not risk a second appearance in Parliament, attended upon by a man whose reputation was discredited in the world of civil engineering.

How far it was a matter of policy and how far a matter of chance that the Rennies were appointed to supplant Stephenson in the new survey is an interesting question. Sir John Rennie gave the following account of the appointment.[27] ' . . . The late Earl of Lonsdale, then Lord Lowther . . . knowing me from my connection with the London Bridge and with Whitehaven Harbour . . . asked my opinion about the proposed new system and whether I thought it likely to succeed. I told him frankly that I thought it would. His Lordship replied, I think so too . . ., and he offered me the post of engineer to the Manchester and Liverpool Railway . . . I replied that my brother and myself would be happy to undertake it, provided that we did not interfere with Mr Stephenson or any other engineer who had previously been employed. Lord Lonsdale said he would arrange all that with the company and my brother and myself were accordingly appointed engineers in chief . . .'

It is difficult to envisage a starker contrast than that between the new engineering staff and the old. In virtually every respect the Rennies and Stephenson were at opposite poles. Their father had been one of Britain's most distinguished civil engineers.[28] His practice had covered canal and harbour work, land drainage and bridges, in addition to which he had carried on an extensive business in mechanical engineering. Early in his career he had attended Edinburgh University and thereafter maintained a close interest in the theoretical aspects of civil engineering. On his death in 1821 his two sons, George and John, continued the practice.

It has traditionally been assumed that George was mainly responsible for the mechanical engineering side of the business, and subsequently his name has tended to be associated with developments in marine engineering. Recently, however, it has been shown[29] that he was closely involved in bridge design, and it may be the case that he was equal partner with his brother John in a number of ventures. Of a somewhat less robust constitu-

tion, he was ill suited to the fieldwork of civil engineering. In consequence it was to John that the task of developing his father's civil engineering contracts fell,[30] the most demanding being the completion of the new London Bridge. His experience of Thames bridges was already extensive, as under his father he had supervised the erection of the Southwark Bridge, a cast-iron structure, and the Waterloo Bridge, which comprised nine masonry arches, each with a span of 120 ft.

In employing the Rennies it seems likely that the Railway Company wished to restore its image as much as to take on more competent engineering staff. Lowther's part in this episode is somewhat enigmatic, for he appears to have had no direct relationship with the Company.[31] He was one of the members attending the committee which advocated the reintroduction of the Bill, and was also proposed as an alternative chairman for the parliamentary committee. Rennie, however, in the account quoted above, gives the impression that Lowther possessed the power to offer the post without recourse to the Railway board. It is possible, therefore, that he had received prior authority from them.

In the event, John Rennie seems to have played little part in the execution of the new survey. The fieldwork was carried out by Charles Blacker Vignoles, who, according to his biographer,[32] was given *carte blanche* by the Rennies. '. . . The engineers evidence distinctly implies that the actual surveys, sections and general profile of the new line were his own . . .'

Vignoles's background again illustrates the disparity between Stephenson and his assistants and their newly appointed replacements. He was the grandson of William Hutton, Professor of Mathematics at the Woolwich Academy. Through singular circumstances he had been enlisted into the army at the age of three. His professional career in that capacity being somewhat limited by his age, he was brought up and educated by his grandfather, who was responsible for his earliest knowledge of surveying and civil engineering. At a later date when active in his military role and beginning his engineering career, he was asked from whom had he learnt his engineering, and he replied, '. . . that his grandfather, Mr Hutton was responsible . . .'.

The end of the war reduced Vignoles to half-pay status, and this prompted him to seek other employment as a civil engineer and surveyor. In 1817 he moved to Charleston, Florida, and for the next six years carried out extensive surveys in that state. In 1823, the year Hutton died, he returned to England. Hutton's posthumous influence enabled him to obtain work with the Rennies, but by 1825 he had built up a substantial independent practice.

Vignoles's new route differed substantially from that proposed by Stephenson.[33] From Kenyon to Liverpool Stephenson's line had followed a more northerly course skirting Knowsley Park, seat of Lord Sefton, to approach Liverpool from Bootle. Vignoles, briefed to avoid opposition, was forced to pursue a more difficult approach involving extensive tunnelling and the use of rope-worked inclines operated by steam winding-engines. Beyond Liverpool heavier engineering and earthworks were necessary, and two further inclined planes were proposed. Significantly, the crossing of Chat Moss was retained, for, as John Rennie makes clear in his autobiography, the Rennies regarded it as no great obstacle.

Vignoles's approach to Manchester was parallel to Stephenson's but about a mile to the north. The crossing of the Irwell, the Medlock, and the incursions over the lands of Miss Byrom and Mrs Atherton, were abandoned. Instead the line followed the course of the Regents Road to turn north at Oldfield Lane and terminate in Salford, below the walls of the New Bailey prison.

Although four miles shorter, the new route was in several respects an inferior alternative. Stephenson's ability to select the best overall course for a prospective line with only the most cursory inspection of the terrain is noted by both Smiles and Rolt. However, in the case of the Liverpool and Manchester Railway this advantage had been forfeited by his indifference towards the execution of the survey.

For the examination of the 1826 Bill the opposing and defending counsel were identical to those of 1825. On behalf of the Company the engineering case was presented by Vignoles and George Rennie. John was absent throughout the proceedings due to a fall into the caisson at London Bridge. Under cross-examination the urbane Vignoles was unshaken. Supporting expert witnesses included Josias Jessop, who had extensive canal and railway experience, and Alexander Nimmo, a notable Scottish surveyor and road and bridge builder, who proved particularly useful to the Company when questioned about the possibility of crossing Chat Moss.

Deprived of the openings Stephenson had afforded them, the opposition could only reiterate the remaining aspects of the case they had presented twelve months earlier. The success of the 1826 Bill is indicative of the extent to which Stephenson was responsible for the failure of that presented in 1825.

In view of all this, Stephenson's reappointment as Company engineer following the successful passage of

the Bill is difficult to explain satisfactorily. In John Rennie's words,[34] '. . . after the passing of the bill, my brother and myself prepared working drawings and estimates for carrying the work into effect and we naturally expected to be appointed the executive engineers after having so much labour and anxiety . . . The executive committee of the company behaved extremely ill to us . . .'

For reasons which are now no longer evident, Stephenson, though discredited in the eyes of the outside world, retained an important element of support within the Company. Moss, convinced of his worth, had written,[35] '. . . No one can be more satisfied than I am that you deserved very different treatment than you met with from Mr Alderson. Your talents are of a much more valuable nature than that of a witness in the House of Commons . . .' Both Joseph Sandars, a director, and Booth also maintained faith in him.

To some extent Alderson's searching cross-examination had unjustly caricatured Stephenson's shortcomings. Despite his performance before the parliamentary committee, his reputation was founded on a number of very real achievements, achievements which had attracted the support of all his previous patrons and promoters. It must be stressed, however, that in the main these had been connected with the steam engine, the steam locomotive and with permanent-way development. His previous railway building work had made only limited demands upon his talents as a civil engineer. The Hetton Railway, the Killingworth line and the Stockton and Darlington Railway were in the small-scale tradition of the colliery plateway, but the Liverpool and Manchester was a project much more akin to the world of canal-building.

The situation may also have been complicated by the directors' lack of previous experience in handling a civil engineering undertaking. Their views of what constituted an appropriate organisational structure for carrying out the works ran directly counter to those of the Rennies. Against the pyramidal organisation developed by Telford and the senior Rennie, with its chain of direct accountability, the directors were proposing that the resident engineer should be their own appointment. It was their opinion that 'it is not advisable that the Rennies should be engaged as sole principle engineers'.[36]

On 17 June 1826[37] George Rennie attended the committee and stated the terms on which they would accept the contract. As chief engineers they would visit the site six times a year, each for seven to ten days. The site work would be carried out by a resident engineer for whose acts they would be responsible; necessarily his appointment should be in their hands. They had no objection to the directors calling in a consultant engineer, for instance Jessop or Telford, but they insisted that he be a member of the Society of Engineers.[38] Finally, they would not consent in any way to be associated with Rastrick or George Stephenson in connection with the civil engineering works, although they had no objection to Stephenson having charge of the Motive Power Department. As far as the Rennies were concerned, the crux was the directors' refusal to confine Stephenson to the areas of his greatest experience, although there was also an element of professional exclusiveness involved.

At the next board[39] the directors decided that the

Rennies' terms were unacceptable, and resolved to appoint Jessop as consulting engineer, with either Rastrick or Stephenson as principal engineer, pending suitable testimonials. On 3 July 1826 Stephenson was appointed engineer at a salary of £800 per annum and on the stipulation that he remain on site for nine months of the year whilst the work was in progress.

In fact, for all the Rennies' insistence that they should have the appointment of the resident engineer, the directors had already commissioned Vignoles to begin work on laying out the line, an appointment to which the Rennies no doubt agreed to but to which Stephenson certainly did not. It was not long before Stephenson found a pretext to have Vignoles dismissed.

Notes

[1] Henry Booth, *An Account of the Liverpool and Manchester Railway*, 1830, rpr. Cass, 1969, p. 16.

[2] Charles Hadfield and Gordon Biddle, *The Canals of North West England*, vol. 1, David and Charles, 1970, p. 109.

[3] Committee on the Liverpool and Manchester Railroad, *Proceedings of the Committee of the House of Commons on the Liverpool and Manchester Railroad Bill*, 1825, pp. 148 ff., 211 ff.

[4] *Ibid.*, p. 380.

[5] Letter from George Stephenson to Michael Longridge, 11 April 1824, Library of the Institute of Mechanical Engineers.

[6] Samuel Smiles, *The Life of George Stephenson, Railway Engineer*, Murray, 1857, p. 128.

[7] L. T. C. Rolt, *George and Robert Stephenson*, Longman, 1960, rpr. Pelican Books, 1978, p. 124.

[8] *Ibid.*, p. 103.

[9] N. W. Webster, *Joseph Locke – Railway Revolutionary*, Allen & Unwin, 1970, p. 33.

[10] Diaries and MS Autobiography of Thomas Longridge Gooch, Library of the Institute of Civil Engineers.

[11] Rolt, *George and Robert Stephenson*, p. 91.

[12] W. W. Tomlinson, *The North Eastern Railway*, 1914, rpr. David and Charles, 1967, p. 116.

[13] Rolt, *George and Robert Stephenson*, p. 109.

[14] Elijah Galloway's *History and Progress of the Steam Engine*, 1829, was one of the first treatises on the steam engine.

[15] Article on 'Netlam Giles', *D.N.B.*, xxi, p. 347, and *Transactions of the Thoresby Society*, 'Leeds maps and mapmakers', vol. 47, 1958, p. 133.

[16] Autobiography of *Sir John Rennie, F.R.S.*, E. and F. N. Spon, 1875, p. 5.

[17] Committee on the Liverpool and Manchester Railway, *op. cit.*, p. 381.

[18] *Ibid.*, p. 421.

[19] *Ibid.*, p. 422.

[20] See also Telford's comments contained in his *Report to the Commissioners for the Loan of Exchequer Bills with Observations in Reply by the Directors of the said Railway*, 1829, copy in Library of the University of London. Telford expressed misgivings about slope stability at this time, particularly with respect to the Sankey embankment. Stabilisation was not achieved here until 1833.

[21] Committee on the Liverpool and Manchester Railroad, *op. cit.*, Preamble to the Bill.

[22] *Ibid.*, pp. 258 ff.

[23] *Ibid.*, pp. 381 ff.

[24] R. E. Carlson, *The Liverpool and Manchester Railway Project, 1821–1831*, David and Charles, 1969, pp. 140 ff.

[25] *Ibid.*

[26] Booth, *An Account of the Liverpool and Manchester Railway*, p. 18.

[27] Autobiography of *Sir John Rennie*, p. 236.

[28] C. T. G. Boucher, *John Rennie, 1761–1821*, Manchester University Press, 1963.

[29] J. J. Hopkins, *A Span of Bridges*, David and Charles, 1970, p. 56.

[30] Autobiography of *Sir John Rennie*, p. 173.

[31] Carlson, *Liverpool and Manchester Railway Project*, pp. 156–7.

[32] Olinthus J. Vignoles, *Life of C. B. Vignoles, F.R.S., Soldier and Civil Engineer*, Longmans, 1889, p. 110.

[33] Maps, Plans and Sections Book deposited with the 1826 Bill, now at the Public Record Office.

[34] Autobiography of *Sir John Rennie*, p. 238.

[35] Letter from Moss to Stephenson, 13 July 1825, now in the Crow collection of the Library of the Institute of Mechanical Engineers.

[36] Minutes of the Board of Directors, 9 June 1826.

[37] *Ibid.*, 17 June 1826.

[38] The Society of Engineers was an early professional association for consulting engineers only. The I.C.E. followed later.

[39] Minutes of the Board of Directors, 3 July 1826.

Chapter II

The site of the terminus

One of the more unfortunate compromises necessitated by the failure of the 1825 Bill involved the removal of the terminus of the line from Manchester to Salford. It has been shown that much of the opposition's case rested upon Stephenson's confused notions of exactly how he intended to carry the line to its termination.

The general plan of 1825 for the course of the line was highly advantageous to the Company. (See map 1.) By crossing the river and penetrating the city the line relieved prospective users from Manchester, whence the bulk of the traffic could be expected to arise, from having to make use of the river bridges. This was particularly significant for the Eccles Bridge, which carried a toll and would have formed one of the main points of access to the town. If the Company succeeded in crossing the river and establishing a Manchester depot there was, of course, nothing to prevent it opening a further depot on the Salford side of the river, thus freeing its customers on both sides from bridge tolls.

The planned Manchester terminal was also well integrated into existing transport facilities. The line lay between Water Street and Deansgate, both improved roads, the latter of which formed the main artery out of Manchester to the south-west. To the west of Water Street and parallel to the railway lay the Mersey and Irwell Navigation, the Old Quay Company, whose warehouses lined the banks of the river, along with those of the other carrying companies using the waterway. The final curve of the Medlock before it entered the Irwell formed the Castlefield Basin of the Bridgewater Canal, into which the Rochdale Canal also discharged. Collectively this area represented the greatest concentration of warehousing in Manchester. With its corresponding infrastructure it could not fail to attract the Railway Company. The Medlock had also acted as a focus for the development of one of Manchester's key cotton manufacturing areas, the growth of which had been particularly dynamic over the previous two decades.[1]

With one critical exception the survey had avoided interfering with existing buildings. The only houses in the area were six dwellings at the junction of Regents Road with Water Street.[2] By terminating the line at Great John Street, Stephenson stopped short of the triangle of buildings enclosed by Quay Street, Water Street and Young Street. It was, therefore, no little irony that the land he had chosen to cross had only shortly before been laid out by Henry Atherton for estate development. By the time the Bill was presented, Atherton had died, but his widow Ann, with Miss Byrom, intended the development to continue.[3] Understandably they did not see the railway, whether on an embankment or in a cutting, as a harmonious neighbour for their genteel dwellings. Nor were their protestations concerning the effects of the steam locomotive without justice. The steamboats which had been employed on the Mersey and Irwell since 1816[4] had given some intimation of the nuisance that could be expected.

Mrs Atherton and Miss Byrom together played a substantial role in opposing the passage of the railway through Manchester, but once again it was to fall to the Mersey and Irwell Navigation Company to lead. Stephenson had chosen to terminate the line on premises owned by the Navigation and used as a slate and timber yard. Because at this stage of the proceedings he had become so evasive, it is difficult to assess whether he put his head in the lion's mouth deliberately or not. Questioned, he had professed to being unaware of the fact that the site belonged to the Navigation Company.[5] Again the loose definition of the survey was turned against him, for he was wholly unsure of the quantity of land to be taken from the Navigation Company and the extent to which it would affect its warehouse premises. All this must have seemed incredibly good fortune to the opposition and their counsel.

In the revised survey Vignoles preferred to forego the advantages of Stephenson's terminus and avoid contact with the propertied or navigation interests of Manchester altogether. His tactical solution took the form of terminating the line on the Salford side of the river.[6] (See map 1.) From a bridge under Oldfield Road the route was planned to curve north-east across open ground to finish below the western walls of the New Bailey prison and against New Bailey Street, which communicated direct with the main bridge over the Irwell into Manchester. It is probable that this course was again a response to the tolls exacted for crossing the Eccles Bridge, for the New Bailey Bridge was toll-free. Apart from the Oldfield Road Bridge, the only major civil engineering work entailed by the revised route would be the crossing of the Manchester Bolton and Bury Canal, which Vignoles planned to achieve at the point were the canal was crossed by Ordsall Lane. A single bridge would thus suffice to carry the railway over both the canal and the road. The site for the station and depot, as far as can be ascertained, was that later occupied by the Salford Station of the Manchester and Bolton Railway.

How completely the Railway Company had resigned itself to abandoning the prospect of a Manchester terminus it is now impossible to say. The Liverpool and Manchester Railway obtained parliamentary sanction on 5 May 1826, but between that date and the end of 1827 little appears to have been accomplished at Manchester. To some extent this can be explained by the emphasis initially placed on the more complex engineering problems. Work on Chat Moss, for instance, began immediately the Bill had passed into law. By mid-June Vignoles had staked out the course of the railway across the Moss, and by 3 July drainage ditches had been extensively laid out. The other major engineering feature of the line, the Liverpool tunnel, also took priority. After an unsuccessful bid by John Foster of Liverpool for the contract, the specification for tender was issued on 25 August 1826, and by 4 September contracts 3, 4 and 5 were let to John Stephenson, George Barker and John Upton to sink shafts and drive the headings.

Even so, the fact that little attempt appears to have been made over the next twelve months to purchase land for the Salford end of the line lends some support to the view that the directors were not enthusiastic about a Manchester station sited within the insalubrious shadow of the New Bailey prison. It is possible that the board saw Vignoles's proposed terminus as a mere device to secure the passage of the Bill. On 31 December 1827,[7] at the weekly board meeting, it was revealed that covert negotiations had been carried on to re-establish the railway on the Manchester side of the river. Some purchase of land had already taken place by this time, but particulars of the transactions have not been recorded.

At the beginning of the September prior to the meeting, the chairman, Charles Lawrence, had received a communication from George Jones of Manchester indicating that an extensive plot of ground belonging to the Old Quay Company, lying on the Salford side of the river and immediately to the south of the Bolton and Bury Canal, was to be offered for sale. This, Jones felt, would make a suitable station site for the railway. Jones already owned land near by which he had previously purchased from the Duchy of Lancaster and with which he had also acquired authority to build a bridge over the Irwell. It was Jones's proposition that, given that the Mersey and Irwell Navigation could hardly be expected to sell the land to the Railway Company except at an exorbitant rate, he should purchase it from the Navigation on the Railway Company's behalf. Knowing that it would wish to bridge the river, he proposed that in return for this discreet service the Railway Company should provide accommodation on its bridge for his traffic. Jones would thus have the use of the bridge without incurring the cost. The Railway Company assented to his proposal and authorised him to offer 4*d* per square yard at twenty years' purchase for

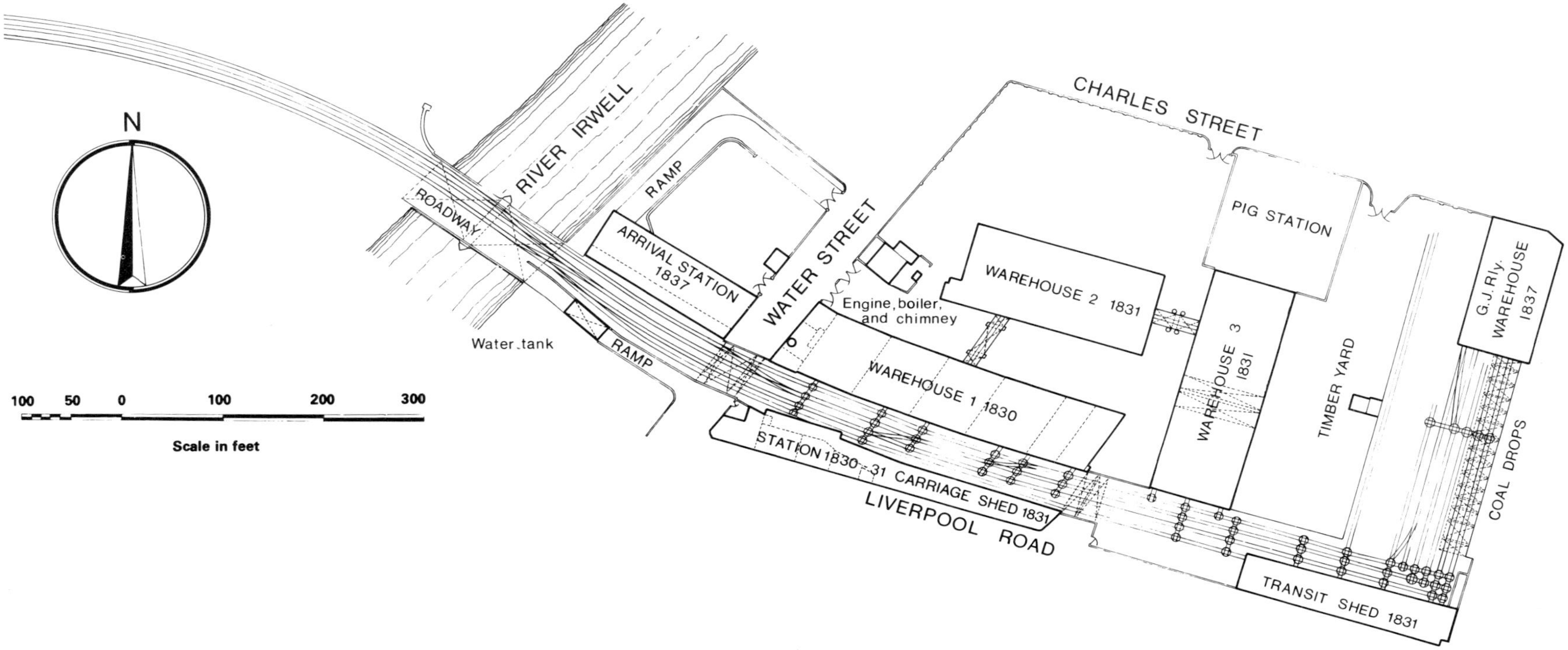

CHARLES STREET

G.J. Rly. WAREHOUSE 1837

COAL DROPS

PIG STATION

TIMBER YARD

WAREHOUSE 3 1831

TRANSIT SHED 1831

WAREHOUSE 2 1831

Engine, boiler, and chimney

WAREHOUSE 1 1830

STATION 1830–31 CARRIAGE SHED 1831

LIVERPOOL ROAD

WATER STREET

RAMP

ARRIVAL STATION 1837

RAMP

Water tank

ROADWAY

RIVER IRWELL

N

Scale in feet

100   50   0   100   200   300

Map 2. General plan of the site.

25,000 square yards of land. Whether the Mersey and Irwell Navigation suspected the origins of the offer or not is unclear, but the negotiations failed and in consequence the Railway Company did not secure the site.

While Jones had been manoeuvring on the Company's behalf, developments had been taking place on the opposite bank of the river, probably in part anticipating the successful acquisition of the Old Quay Company's land. The Railway carrying committee had been informed[8] that a plot of ground on the east bank lying between the warehouses of the Old and the New Quay Companies might be coming on to the market. The parcel in question consisted of about 6,000 square yards partly occupied by a dyeworks. Two of the directors, accompanied by Stephenson, visited the site and, in Lawrence's words, found it '... very desirable ... for the termination of the line and on many accounts preferable to the site near the New Bailey Prison ...'. With the sanction of the board it was purchased for £10,000 subject to a chief rent of £96 per annum.[9] With this foothold in Manchester, the Railway Company felt sufficiently confident to proceed. On 4 February 1828 Lawrence was empowered to open negotiations for the purchase of land with the relevant parties in Manchester. Inevitably the Mersey and Irwell Navigation would be involved, for, as had transpired during the course of the 1825 Bill's progress, it held a virtual monopoly of land on the banks of the river. Lawrence drafted a letter to the Old Quay Company informing it of the Railway Company's intention to apply to Parliament for power to vary the termination of the line at the Manchester end and requesting to know whether the Old Quay Company would be willing to sell such a portion of its land on the west side of the Irwell as might be required by the Railway.

The Old Quay Company agreed to send a deputation to meet Lawrence and Moss. At the next board meeting the two directors reported the result. The Old Quay deputation, although not empowered to negotiate terms, seemed to have been favourably disposed towards the Railway Company and had returned to their board to convey the Railway Company's terms. Three weeeks later further discussions took place between Lawrence and Moss and the Old Quay Company, which by this time had formulated the conditions upon which it would consent to the Railway Company passing through its land in Salford to gain access to its projected station on the east bank of the river . The price of the Navigation's acquiescence was that the Railway Company should make provision on its bridge over the Irwell for the cart traffic of the Navigation Company, allowing access across

the river and down into Water Street; the Old Quay Company should retain the frontage to the railway on both sides from its land in Salford except for a square plot to be purchased by the Railway Company in addition to the area required for the railway itself. The Navigation Company also required a concession at the Liverpool end of the line. Provision was to be made for it to acquire a plot of ground sufficient to construct a warehouse with a 300 square yard ground plan capable of accommodating its own wagons. For this the Navigation Company was to pay the market price. In return the Railway Company was to acquire a quantity of land in Salford not exceeding thirty-seven yards in width along the length of the line of the railway with the addition of the square plot of land referred to above. The price demanded by the Old Quay Company was 1s per square yard chief rent.

These terms on the part of the Navigation Company reflect a considerably altered strategy to that which it had adopted three years earlier. The company would appear by this time to have abandoned any prospect of preventing the Railway achieving its ends. Instead, the opportunity to profit from the new venture may well have presented itself, and this seems to have conditioned its response to the overtures of the Railway Company. The Old Quay Company was fully aware of the potential profitability of carrying and the ownership of warehouses from its own experience.[10] It may be that its negotiations with the Railway Company were conducted against a background of its possible participation in the carrying trade along the line when it was eventually opened. By securing the frontages to the railway in Salford it provided for itself the facility to erect warehouses without having to re-negotiate in less favourable circumstances later. In the same way it had ensured that the Liverpool end of the line remained open to it. With one or two reservations the Railway Company found the terms acceptable, and a further letter was drafted to the Old Quay Company to the effect that, subject to modification of certain clauses affecting the width of the Irwell Bridge, it was prepared to accede.

The Railway also considered it advisable to approach Robert Haldane Bradshaw, Superintendent of the Bridgewater Trust, in order to gain some indication of whether he was disposed to object. On this occasion Gilbert Winter accompanied Moss. Winter,[11] a Manchester wine merchant, had been an early subscriber to the Railway, having taken out shares amounting to £1,333 6s 8d in 1825. A member of the board, he was to play the leading part in the operations of the Railway Company at the Manchester end of the line.

Bradshaw's response was ambiguous.[12] He too, possibly with the added impetus of Lord Stafford's holdings in the Railway Company, appears to have abandoned any prospect of arresting the progress of the line. At first he attempted to persuade the deputation that the New Bailey site was preferable to the proposed alteration. Unable to achieve this, he was forced to concede that the Railway had acted wisely in deciding to cross the river. He would give no binding assurance not to oppose the Bill, but on the other hand he did not seem particularly inclined to do so. The deputation was left with the impression that, in return for his favour, he might require similar accommodation to that granted to the Old Quay Company.[13]

By the end of October 1828 the Railway Company had achieved its most important objective as far as the Manchester end of the line was concerned, in re-establishing itself on the eastern bank of the Irwell. Its stated intention initially had been to confine the railway to the margin of land between Water Street and the river. To make way for the station, the dyeworks of Messrs Rothwell Harrison were to be demolished, giving a cleared area 66 yards deep with about 100 yards of frontage on to Water Street. Increasingly, however, the directors began to be concerned about the restricted depth of the site, and attention turned to the fields on the east side of Water Street, enclosed by Charles Street and Liverpool Road, directly opposite the ground occupied by the dyeworks. Perhaps fortuitously, this land belonged to Mr Gilbert Winter, whose offer of 35,500 square yards for 1s per square yard chief rent was read to the carrying committee on 1 December 1828. The week following the board resolved to acquire the whole plot at 1s per square yard annual rent.[14] It only remained to obtain parliamentary powers to alter the course of the line. (See map 1.) The intention of the board to extend their parliamentary powers was announced at the General Meeting of 3 November 1828, and accordingly on 14 May 1829 by 10 Geo. IV, cap. 35, the Company was empowered to '. . . make such deviations . . . from such part of a piece of land laid out as gardens in the Township of Salford belonging to the Earl of Derby . . . in a south easterly direction . . . through the Township of Salford and across the Irwell, through and upon part of the Township of Manchester and terminating in or near to a certain field lying in the eastwardly side of Water Street and the northwardly side of Liverpool Road and lying between the same street and Charles Street'.

Notes

[1] Sylvia Clarke, unpublished MS on the development of the cotton textile mills in the Medlock Valley area of Manchester, in the possession of Professor D. S. L. Cardwell, University of Manchester Institute of Science and Technology.

[2] Committee on the Liverpool and Manchester Railroad, *Proceedings of the Committee of the House of Commons on the Liverpool and Manchester Railroad Bill,* 1825, Plans and Sections.

[3] John Kellett, *The Impact of Railways on Victorian Cities,* Routledge & Kegan Paul, 1969, p. 154.

[4] Early steamboats with their primitive tank boilers were notorious smoke producers, and much of the early work on smoke prevention was carried out in this context.

[5] Committee on the Liverpool and Manchester Railroad, *op. cit.,* p. 227.

[6] Maps, plans and sections deposited with the 1826 Bill, now at the Public Record Office.

[7] Minutes of the Board of Directors, 31 December 1827.

[8] *Ibid.*

[9] *Ibid.*

[10] Committee on the Liverpool and Manchester Railroad, *op. cit.,* pp. 100 ff.

[11] J. Swindells, *Manchester Streets and Manchester Men,* 1908.

[12] Carlson, *Liverpool and Manchester Railway Project, 1821–31,* pp. 147–8, for a discussion of Bradshaw's position.

[13] Minutes of the Board of Directors, 20 September 1828.

[14] *Ibid.,* 8 December 1828.

Chapter III

The Irwell and Water Street Bridges

The civil engineering on the Liverpool and Manchester Railway far exceeded anything Stephenson had previously attempted. In addition to Chat Moss and the Liverpool tunnel he was called upon to provide over sixty bridges, and in some ways they represent a greater achievement. It is, therefore, relevant to ask upon what basis the designs for these structures were formulated.

Although the basic devices of theoretical analysis had been developed by the beginning of the nineteenth century, there are few documented examples of bridge design rationalised in this way. Among the few recorded instances in which scientific principles are known to have been applied are the Southwark and Waterloo bridges of the elder John Rennie. Generally speaking, builders either drew upon observation of established practice, supplemented by tabulated sets of rules governing proportion, as did Smeaton, or acquired experience in the practice of their craft. Telford, for instance, began his career as a stonemason, an origin common to many bridge engineers and surveyors.

The situation is less clear in the case of Stephenson. His previous lines had demanded little of him as a bridge builder, for the majority of bridges on the Stockton and Darlington Railway had been single semi-circular arches with only limited spans. Of the two river crossings, one had been accomplished in iron and will be discussed later, whilst his part in the design and construction of the other, the masonry bridge over the Skerne, was of only marginal importance.[1] He first suggested an iron bridge, and construction began accordingly. The foundation work was not far advanced before the advice of Ignatius Bonhomi, Surveyor of Bridges for Durham, was sought. When the foundation stone was laid in July 1824 modifications by Bonhomi had already been included in the structure. Eventually the entire work was placed in Bonhomi's hands, and the bulk of the design, now in stone, has been shown to have been his.

Equally, it is difficult to assess the extent to which Stephenson was able to utilise the literature upon the subject. His education was sketchy and the art of writing, acquired late, never came easily to him.[2] Smiles gives the impression that he attained some skill in arithmetic, but the didactic nature of Smiles's work makes his account suspect. Summerside maintains that Stephenson's achievements were limited to the rule of five contained in Tinwall's *Arithmetic*.[3] Rolt, by far the ablest biographer of Stephenson,[4] maintains that he lacked any ability to store theoretical knowledge but relied instead upon mechanical understanding and intuition. It is Rolt's opinion also that Robert Stephenson played a vital role as surrogate

Bridges on the Stockton and Darlington Railway. (*Above left*) the Hummerbeck Bridge of 1823. Now much mutilated, this was formerly one of the best examples of bridge architecture on the line. (*Above right*) Brusselton accommodation bridge. (*Below*) the Skerne Bridge, begun by Stephenson and completed by Bonhomi.

for his father's lack of education. Robert's schooling was vigorously pursued and culminated in six months at Edinburgh University in 1822. Both Smiles and Summerside speak of Robert as one of the principal means by which George gained access to the literature and probably to a large extent the understanding of it. However, there is no direct evidence to show that Robert exerted any influence upon the civil engineering of the Liverpool and Manchester Railway. From 1824 until 1827 he was in South America. Much of the bridgework was well advanced by the time of his return, and thereafter the Newcastle works claimed most of his attention. Nevertheless, he was much closer to the construction of the line after 1827 than he was before.

The preparation of the working drawings for the line was largely assigned to Thomas Longridge Gooch. Although Smiles[5] writes that Stephenson had become proficient in draughtsmanship under his teacher, Wigham, he does not seem to have undertaken any of the drawing work for the Liverpool and Manchester Railway. Gooch's own account of his work at this time[6] describes Stephenson as conveying his intentions verbally or by rough sketches on letter paper. If Gooch was the sole draughtsman for the period of construction, as he claims to have been, he must be credited with the detailed design work for the majority of the structures and, probably, the resolution of many of the problems.

He had been apprenticed to Stephenson in 1823, a few months after Joseph Locke.[7] The terms of his indentures provided for two years' instruction as a 'practical engineer' in the works, followed by four years as a civil engineer. His diaries show that these conditions were closely followed.[8] Until December 1825 he was employed in the works, after which he was transferred to the drawing office and, according to his diary, produced designs for mechanical and civil engineering structures including a plan for the centres of the tunnel on the Canterbury and Whitstable Ralway. With Locke he surveyed for the Newcastle and Carlisle line, producing the plans and sections back at the drawing office. His career with Stephenson was interrupted for four months in 1826 whilst he attended Edinburgh University, in part to extend his mathematical knowledge, the essentials of which had been acquired by evening study under a Mr Thompson. In October 1826 he joined Stephenson on the Liverpool and Manchester Railway as his personal secretary and sole draughtsman.

Gooch's abilities were central to the success of the works, but a great deal also depended upon the execution at site level, and this was the responsibility of the resident engineers, who, after Vignoles's departure, were all nominated by George Stephenson. Joseph Locke, aged twenty-one, controlled the western section, William Allcard, aged seventeen, the middle section and John Dixon, the eldest of the trio at thirty, the eastern end into Manchester. Smiles[9] describes the organisational structure thus:

... The resident engineer was responsible for setting out and overseeing the section under his charge from drawings and specifications compiled at the central drawing office. Below the resident were the sub-engineers, often apprentices or pupils. The final level of responsibility comprised the inspectors of tunnelling and masonry, in most cases experienced workmen. The detailed plans of the works were prepared after consultation with the assistant engineers under whose superintendence they were to be executed. The levels were taken and the work set out by the sub-engineers. The centres of bridges and the moulds for difficult masonry were struck out or tested by them and the inspectors ...

Smiles was writing many years after the construction of the Liverpool and Manchester Railway, and it is doubtful whether Stephenson's operational structure in 1826 was as mature as this. Mills, who inspected the line on behalf of Telford in 1828,[10] found little evidence of such a system and was quick to point out that the residents and Gooch were all still apprentices. In spite of this pervasive lack of experience the engineering staff displayed a high level of innovatory talent, notably in bridge design. Most remarkable were the skew bridges, of which there were sixteen by 1830.

Prior to the coming of the railway skew bridges were uncommon. Early canal engineers preferred to avoid

One of the small occupation bridges towards Liverpool. The design is frequently repeated along the line.

them, since, when built by traditional techniques, they were unstable. The first effective attempt to build a skew bridge that correctly contained the forces imposed upon it was by William Chapman, who in 1789 had built three on the Kildare Canal.[11] Unlike previous attempts at skewed crossings, these bridges employed a system by which the bedding planes of the arch stones were placed at 90° to the line of thrust. In a conventional arch the bedding plane of the arch stones lies parallel to the abutments and meets the line of thrust at 90°. If the arch is skew and an arrangement similar to that of a conventional arch is followed, the line of thrust which runs parallel to the face of the arch intercepts the bedding planes at an oblique angle, and beyond a certain limit failure will occur. For the bedding planes to occupy a position normal to the line of thrust they must make a right angle with the face of the arch and with successive thrust lines across the soffit. In its true form this involves tapering masonry courses which, whilst mechanically correct, are

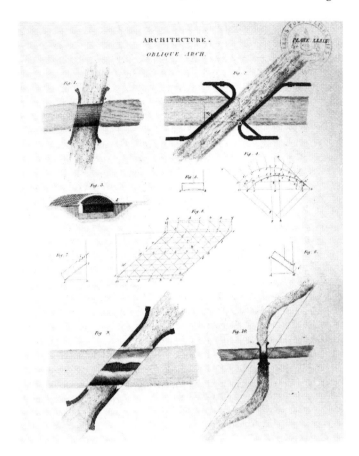

Plate from Rees' *Cyclopedia* of 1814, showing Chapman's derivation of the skew arch.

The Rainhill skew bridge. With a 54 ft. span it was the largest skew bridge after the Irwell Bridge. (*Above*) intrados of the Rainhill skew bridge, and (*below*) Bury's print.

more complex from a constructional point of view. In nineteenth-century Britain the most common approach to the problem was to reduce the degree of obliquity of the arch courses to the thrust line to an acceptable level whilst retaining uniform arch stones. This was popularly known as the spiral method, in which the courses of the arch stones could be envisaged as a square-section screw thread winding around the cylinder of the arch. Chapman's design, explained in Rees' *Cyclopedia* of 1814,[12] divided the developed plan of the arch into a grid and superimposed the course lines upon this by diagonals bisecting the grid squares. For the purposes of construction this plan was transferred on to the centring and the arch courses were laid out accordingly to the diagonals marked upon the surface of the lagging boards.

In 1827 Peter Nicholson[13] published an alternative method of describing the spiral line which had the advantage of allowing the blockwork of the arch to be shaped away from the centres. Circumstantial evidence, however, indicates that Chapman's, rather than Nicholson's, method was employed on the Liverpool and Manchester Railway. Even if the engineers on the Railway had ready access to Nicholson's book it is probable that they were more familiar with Rees' *Cyclopedia*. Furthermore, several of the bridges were complete by mid-1828,[14] although the design for the largest, the Rainhill Bridge, was not finished until the end of that year. It is also noteworthy that the arches for most of the bridges are of brick rather than stone, a material that lent itself more to Chapman's method than Nicholson's, which was primarily aimed at masons. Finally, C. R. Condor's account[15] of Robert Stephenson's mode of skew-arch construction on the London and Birmingham Railway describes features similar to those of Chapman. Here the centring of the arch was covered with sheeting upon which the lines for the courses were marked with a flexible straight edge. Condor believed this method to be of Robert Stephenson's own devising. He also refers to the fact that Robert considered it necessary to construct a wooden model of some of the bridges before embarking on the job itself. This is known to have been done on two other occasions on lines associated with the Stephensons: at the Gaunless Bridge on the Haggar Leases branch of the Stockton and Darlington Railway designed by Thomas Storey in 1829 and on the Rainhill Bridge, both masonry arches.

It was against this background that the Irwell Bridge was designed. Contemporary writers spared it no more than passing notice, despite the fact that it was the most complex on the line. In 1825 the initiative in selecting the site and the method of crossing the river lay with Stephenson. The result was a projected crossing-point with a highly favourable combination of assets:[16] the narrowest point of the river, an outcrop of rock capable of sustaining the foundation and abutment thrusts, and a high bank level. (See map 1.) In contrast, his later choice was circumscribed by external factors. The location of the crossing was dictated by Vignoles's route and involved an embanked approach, whilst the availability of bank space demanded a sharp curve from Oldfield Road. (See map 2.) The form of the bridge was also subject to the demands of the Navigation Company.

In February 1829 an agreement[17] was entered into between the Railway and the Navigation Company whereby the latter agreed to sell land to the former and allow it to interfere with the bed and banks of the river. In return for this the Navigation Company was to be provided with an 18 ft. cartway across the bridge. In order that navigation should remain unimpeded, it was required that the bridge have a headroom of 29 ft. and that a minimum waterway of 63 ft. be provided on either side of the piers, with an 8 ft. towpath on the western bank.

The outline design for the bridge was ready by September 1828, but the enabling Act which gave statutory force to the agreement was not passed until May 1829.[18] Between these dates some discussion took place as to the expediency of building the remaining bridges by single contract rather than by the system which had previously prevailed.[19] Stephenson's method of contracting had been heavily criticised by Mills and Telford.[20] The contracts had been let piecemeal, often on a very informal basis with only a verbal undertaking between Stephenson and the parties concerned, the latter providing labour only. This arrangement had been used on the Stockton and Darlington, but on the much larger Liverpool and Manchester Railway it entailed grave risks. The directors seemed to have taken the reproaches of Telford to heart, for in May 1829 the Irwell Bridge was advertised for single contract in newspapers across the country. The advertisement stated that the bridge was to be of two arches, with an exterior of solid ashlar and arches of brick.[21] The contractor was to find the materials and the centres, scaffolding and coffer-dam.

The successful tender was awarded to J. B. Brockbank and Alexander Fyfe, who quoted £1 19s 6d per cubic yard for the ashlar, 15s 7½d for the rubble and £1 1s 1d for the brickwork.[22] Brockbank first appears in the Manchester directories in 1822 as a slate merchant, but not until 1829 did he include stone in his listing.[23] Whether he also acted as a mason is not indicated before 1830. The directories make no mention of his association with Fyfe, which implies that the partnership was formed exclusively for the Irwell Bridge.

Fyfe had come from Darlington with Stephenson.[24] He was a Scot whose father had worked on the construction of the Caledonian Canal. In June 1824 Fyfe had joined Stephenson on the Stockton and Darlington to work on the foundations of the Gaunless Bridge. A brief biography claims that he was chief designer and draughtsman on the Liverpool and Manchester, responsible for the Edge Hill tunnel and the Sankey Viaduct, but offers no real evidence to support this. When Mills visited the site he was superintendent under Allcard, and Scott Walker lists him as assistant to Holkyard on the Sankey Viaduct. His alliance with Brockbank probably implies a pairing of technical knowledge with a supplier of materials.

It seems that initially the bridge was to follow the style of the Winton Road Bridge, with brick arches and stone

The Winton Road Bridge. (*Above*) the skewed arch, upon which the first design for the Irwell Bridge appears to have been based. The voussoirs are of brick, whilst the exterior and quoins are of stone. (*Below*) the stone exterior encloses a brick skew arch. The curved wing walls and railings are original.

facings. This bridge had a span of 31 ft., half that proposed for the Irwell Bridge. In June Jesse Hartley, the engineer of the Liverpool docks, who had acted as consultant on the Sankey Viaduct, was consulted again by Sandars over the practicability of a brick arch of 60 ft. span.[25] Hartley felt that this could be achieved provided the workmanship and the materials were adequate.

The date when work started is not recorded, but the contractors were in trouble almost immediately. The coffer-dam leaked copiously and after lengthy delays the situation was only brought under control by the use of steam pumps. The directors' report for March 1830 announced that the piers and abutments on the banks were complete but that the wet pier had still to be started. The outlook was brighter the following month, for the *Manchester Guardian*[26] reported that the coffer-dam was now dry and the workmen were engaged in levelling the rock on the bed of the river for the pier, 8 ft. below water level.

Further setbacks followed. In the last week of April[27] a boat which had been used for ferrying the masons from one side of the river to the other capsized and twelve men were drowned. An inventory of the dead indicates the origins of the work force. Of the masons, three came from Scotland and two more from Durham. Only one was local, from Bolton, but most of the labourers came from near by. Fifteen days later the pier was two feet above the water and the centres were ready for placing.[28] The arches which were about to be raised, however, were not those advertised in the notice of tender. Between July, when Hartley gave his opinion, and the raising of the first arch it had decided not to employ brick for the voussoirs but to use stone instead. This change may have been part of a larger-scale alteration to plans not recorded during the period of construction.

After the completion of the bridge Brockbank attempted to gain some redress for the extra work involved beyond that specified in the contract.[29] Hartley was called in to arbitrate and included in his estimates of the extra work done several items of wastage caused by the tardy alteration of the bridge from a square to a skew plan, an alteration perhaps designed to relieve the curve into the depot, which even after completion was eleven chains radius. How such a radical alteration could have been incorporated in the already well advanced bridge masonry it is difficult to say.

Whatever the case, the first arch centre was in place on 1 July,[30] and nineteen days later the arch was keyed. The second centre was placed and sheeted on 15 July and by the end of August a locomotive had passed over the

Whiston Road Bridge (*above left*). The architectural details are repeated on the Irwell Bridge. Construction was complete by mid-1829.

Centre pier of the Irwell Bridge (*above right*). The rustication is reminiscent of the Winton Road Bridge.

Transition between the Irwell Bridge masonry and the brick viaduct (*left*). This well illustrates the change of plan in favour of a masonry bridge.

The masonry bridge over the Irwell (*below*), showing also the water tower: one of the few contemporary views of this bridge, none of which is wholly accurate. *Manchester Public Libraries*

bridge on temporary tracks.[31] This much had only been achieved by great exertions on the part of the contractors, including the introduction of night shifts. Brockbank ended up badly out of pocket and subsequently engaged in lengthy negotiations with the Railway Company to reimburse himself for the losses on the coffer-dam, the realignment and the night work involved. With Hartley as arbitrator he eventually settled for a further £2,030, the total cost of the bridge having been £20,000, four times that estimated by Stephenson in 1825.

The need to conciliate external interests was to have a decisive influence upon the form of the Water Street bridge. Water Street separated the Manchester landfall of the Irwell Bridge from the area designated as the site for the depot, and to cross it a bridge was essential. The 1826 Act included a *caveat* which stipulated that when crossing a public highway the arches of the railway bridge should have a minimum clearance of 15 ft. width, and 16 ft. headroom. Similar provisions were expected from the 1829 Extension of Powers Act. On 2 March 1829[32] Mr Bellhouse and Mr Warren, Surveyors of Highways for Manchester, attended the board and indicated that they considered 16 ft. headroom insufficient. The board was willing to negotiate, and Stephenson was instructed to accompany the Surveyors to the site and see whether a satisfactory arrangement might be arrived at.

In the meantime a public meeting had been held which resulted in a resolution informing the Company[33] that opposition to the Bill might be expected unless minimum dimensions of 24 ft. span and clearances of 17 ft. at the crown of the road and 15 ft. at the kerbside were conformed to. The board was not to be coerced, and replied that it felt itself under no obligation to treat with the parties in view of the fact that negotiations with the Surveyors were proceeding. Nevertheless, it offered to discuss the matter if the petitioners desired. This magnanimity succeeded in deflating the would-be opponents, who, along with the Highway Surveyors, were present at the next meeting '. . . disclaiming any hostility of feeling . . .' and being '. . . present in a spirit of accommodation . . .'. In fact the board had already conceded the point. The 1829 Act provided that the bridge was to have a span of 24 ft. and a clear height of 17 ft. over the whole width of the roadway. Two footpaths were to be provided, each 6 ft. wide and with 12 ft. headroom, separated from the roadway by piers of a maximum width of 2 ft. The railway was to be concealed by a parapet not less than 6 ft. above the level of the rails.

The Company's engineer was thus confronted with one of the classic problems of railway bridge engineering. To the statutory minimum construction depth of 17 ft. he was required to add the rise of the arch, if such were employed, the structural depth and the level of the permanent way materials, thus establishing a rail level far in excess of that which prevailed on the Irwell Bridge only seventy yards away. To adjust these levels, Stephenson could have adopted one of a number of solutions. He could have lowered the road level, but this was unlikely to meet with the approval of the Highway Surveyors. Alternatively, he could have regraded the track levels, but this would have been highly disruptive to the completed works and would also have given rise to problems in planning the depot. Some advantage might have been gained by using a segmental or semi-elliptical arch, but this approach involved engineering problems. The crossing would have necessitated a skewed arch, at that time

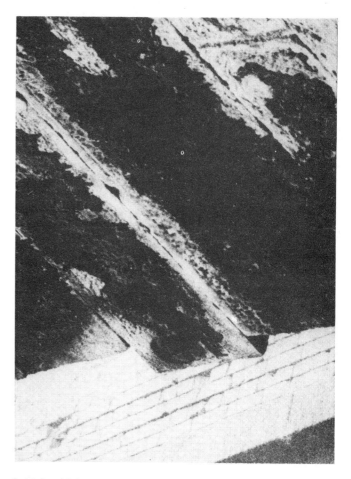

Initials of John Dixon, resident engineer for the eastern end of the line, under the keystone on the western arch of the Irwell Bridge. The other keystone carries the initials G.S.

not considered a practical proposition for a semi-elliptical arch. In addition the shallower arches would have occasioned greater horizontal thrusts at abutment level, with consequently heavier pier construction and foundations. The final alternative was to maintain a constant construction depth of 17 ft. by means of a level beam bridge. All the circumstances favoured this last solution.

Stephenson is known to have considered two designs for the crossing of Water Street, but his eventual choice was a cast-iron girder bridge. He could equally have adopted timber, but certain factors may be supposed to have prompted him to choose iron. As a mechanical engineer he had built not only locomotives but stationary steam engines, possibly some of the largest in the country at the time. To this experience of iron must be added his work on the development of rails, which both familiarised him with the properties of wrought and cast iron and drew him into loaded beam theory. That he was confident of the suitability of iron is attested by the Gaunless Bridge, which Tomlinson credits to him.[34] This four-span lenticular truss carried the Stockton and Darlington Railway over the Gaunless river and was completed in 1824. The distribution of cast and wrought iron components gives some indication of Stephenson's knowledge of the structural properties of each at that time.

Most important of all was his friendship with William Fairbairn, which went back to 1803, when Fairbairn was a pitwright at Percy Main Colliery and Stephenson a banksman at Willington Quay. By the mid-1820s Fairbairn was one of the country's leading engineers. Much of his reputation stemmed from his success as a builder of fireproof mills, in which he employed a system of cast-iron beams supporting brick segmental arch floors. The cast-iron beam was developed almost exclusively as a result of the evolution of the fireproof textile mill. By the second decade of the nineteenth century the form of beam most extensively used for structural purposes consisted of a inverted T cross-section, the flange of which provided support for the brick arch floors. Although the beam section had evolved largely in response to the support conditions necessary for a brick arch, the inverted T section possessed structural properties which suited the characteristics of cast iron. The form was, however, empirical rather then scientific in origin, and room for improvement remained. In the early 1820s Eaton Hodgkinson, a Manchester physicist, began to investigate possible improvements in the form of cast-iron beams. His work drew the attention of the Manchester engineer Peter Ewart, who induced William Fairbairn and his

Stephenson's iron bridge over the river Gaunless, now preserved at the National Railway Museum, York.

partner James Lillie to accommodate Hodgkinson at their Manchester foundry and make available to him their testing facilities.

In order to appreciate the significance of Hodgkinson's work certain features of beam theory must be understood. They can be conveniently explained by taking the case of a rectangular-section beam freely supported at the ends only, with its greatest depth standing vertically. A load concentrated at mid-span will cause the beam to deflect and assume the form of a curve. The upper and lower edges of the beam will be curves of lesser and greater radii, so that the circumferences to which they correspond will be lesser and greater. Effectively the upper edge will have been compressed and the lower edge subjected to tensile stress. At a point intermediate between the two the compressional stresses will be supplanted by tensile stresses, and this point will have neutral status: the neutral axis. In any beam the resistance to deflection is proportional to the square of the depth, so the material located farthest from the neutral axis is more effective in resisting deflection than that closer to the neutral axis. If a material responds equally to tensile and compressive stresses, the ideal section will consist of a vertical web with equal flanges attached to the top and bottom: the familiar I section of a steel joist. This had been proposed by Tredgold in the 1820s as the ideal section for a cast-iron beam but entailed the erroneous assumption that cast iron displayed an identical response to tensile and compressive stresses.

Inverted T section beams in a Leeds warehouse. This was the earliest cross-sectional form for cast-iron beams.

The Water Street Bridge. *(Right, above)* Crane's lithograph, the most reliable view of this structure, nevertheless contains inaccuracies. *Liverpool Public Libraries (Right)* viewed from the north. Unlike the Crane lithograph this view shows all the columns as fluted. The gable of the warehouse is also shown, prior to the construction of the boiler and engine houses which later powered the hoisting machinery. *Manchester Public Libraries (Below)* this view exaggerates the span but is correct in the details it depicts. The roof and gable of the warehouse are incorrectly shown. The chimney is that of the boiler supplying steam to the hoist engines. Rothwell Harrison's dyeworks occupy the left background. *Manchester Public Libraries*

Hodgkinson's experiments involved testing to destruction cast-iron specimens of varying cross-section and noting the manner in which they failed. This enabled him to conclude that cast iron underwent tensile failure considerably earlier than compressional failure occurred. To produce a beam proportioned to fail simultaneously from both stresses, the bottom flange required a sectional area six times greater than that of the top flange. To conform with the nature of the load–span relationship, the beam should have a maximum cross-section at a point farthest from the supports and diminish in section towards the supports according to a parabolic curve. In the Hodgkinson beam this involved a web, the upper edge of which was of parabolic profile, and flanges of parabolic plan.

In the printed account of his work[35] Hodgkinson states that Stephenson was present while a number of the experiments were taking place and had expressed his intention to use the new beam form in his Water Street Bridge. On 7 December 1829[36] Stephenson produced for the board a design for the bridge over Water Street but stated that he had an alternative plan which was not quite ready. Almost certainly the latter was that which embodied the results of Hodgkinson's work. It is equally certain that both Hodgkinson and Fairbairn played some part in the design of the structure. Fairbairn's later fame owed much to his advocacy and use of the Hodgkinson beam. The earliest mill by Fairbairn known to have included the new beams was Orrell's Mill, Stockport, of 1834. Prior to that he is said to have designed a mill in Macclesfield using the beams, but the *Manchester Guar-*

dian in May 1830 indicated that construction had not started at that date. The evidence is that the Water Street Bridge was the first application of the new section, for on 12 April 1830 the outer piers were nearly complete.

At first it was intended that the main beams should be supported by a stone wall separating the footways from the road, the footways being arched over in brick.[37] At the request of the Highway Surveyors this plan was abandoned in favour of two rows of columns. Most accounts of the bridge, including one of 1904,[38] describe the columns as being of stone, and masons are known to have worked upon the structure. Wishaw, however, states them to be of cast iron.[39] The superstructure of ironwork was cast by Fairbairn and Lillie. The writings of both Fairbairn[40] and Hodgkinson[41] illustrate a section of one of the main beams which had been tested to an ultimate load of 110 tons.[42]

In 1893, as part of a programme of cast girder bridge replacement following the failure of two such structures in 1882 and 1891, plans were drawn up for the replacement of the Water Street Bridge. These plans, showing both the earlier bridge and its replacement, survive and have been used along with photographs taken at the time of demolition in 1905 for the reconstruction drawing.[43] The following description is based upon the drawings.

The road span of the bridge was 24 ft. 6 in., while the footpath spans were 6 ft. The square length was 50 ft. and the angle of skew 39°. At the crown of the road the clearance was 16 ft. 10 in. Between the parapets at rail level the width of the way was 48 ft. The five main beams had a

South elevation of the Water Street Bridge prior to demolition in 1905. *Chris Makepeace*

Demolition about to commence on the Water Street Bridge in 1905. *Chris Makepeace*

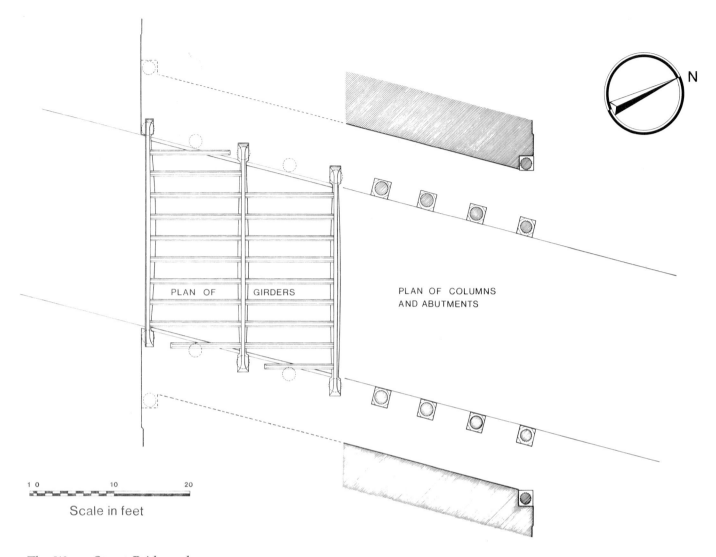

PLAN OF   GIRDERS

PLAN OF COLUMNS
AND ABUTMENTS

N

1 0   10   20

Scale in feet

The Water Street Bridge: plan.

clear span of 24 ft. 9 in. and were placed at 13 ft. 5 in. centres. Both the flange plans and longitudinal profile were parabolic, with a mid-span section of 2 ft. 3 in. total depth over flanges. The bottom flange was 3 in. × 9 in. and the top flange 6 in. × 1¾ in., a ratio of just over five to one. The web appears to have been constant thickness at 2 in. A narrow rib positioned 1 ft. above the bottom flange ran parallel to it for the length of the beam, whilst the upper surface of the bottom flange had lugs cast in. These located the secondary beams, spanning between the main beams at 2 ft. 9 in. intervals. The cross-sectional profile accords with Hodgkinson's form, but the plan and the elevation were of parallel profile. The overall depth was 1 ft. 3 in. with a bottom flange 9 in. × 1¼ in. and the

top flange about 4 in. × ¾ in. The secondary beams carried brick arches with a rise of 4 in. There is no evidence of tie-bars between either the secondary beams or the principals. The footways were brick-arched, concealed behind a false ceiling.

The girder superstructure was supported by two rows of nine columns which tapered from 1 ft. 9 in. below the echinus to 2 ft. at the base, rising from a plinth. The total height over plinth and capital was 12 ft. 6 in. The entablature separating the columns from the girders appears to have been of stone. It performed no structural role with respect to the main spans, the girders being located over alternate columns. The terminal jack arches of the main span abutted the spandrel masonry of the side arches.

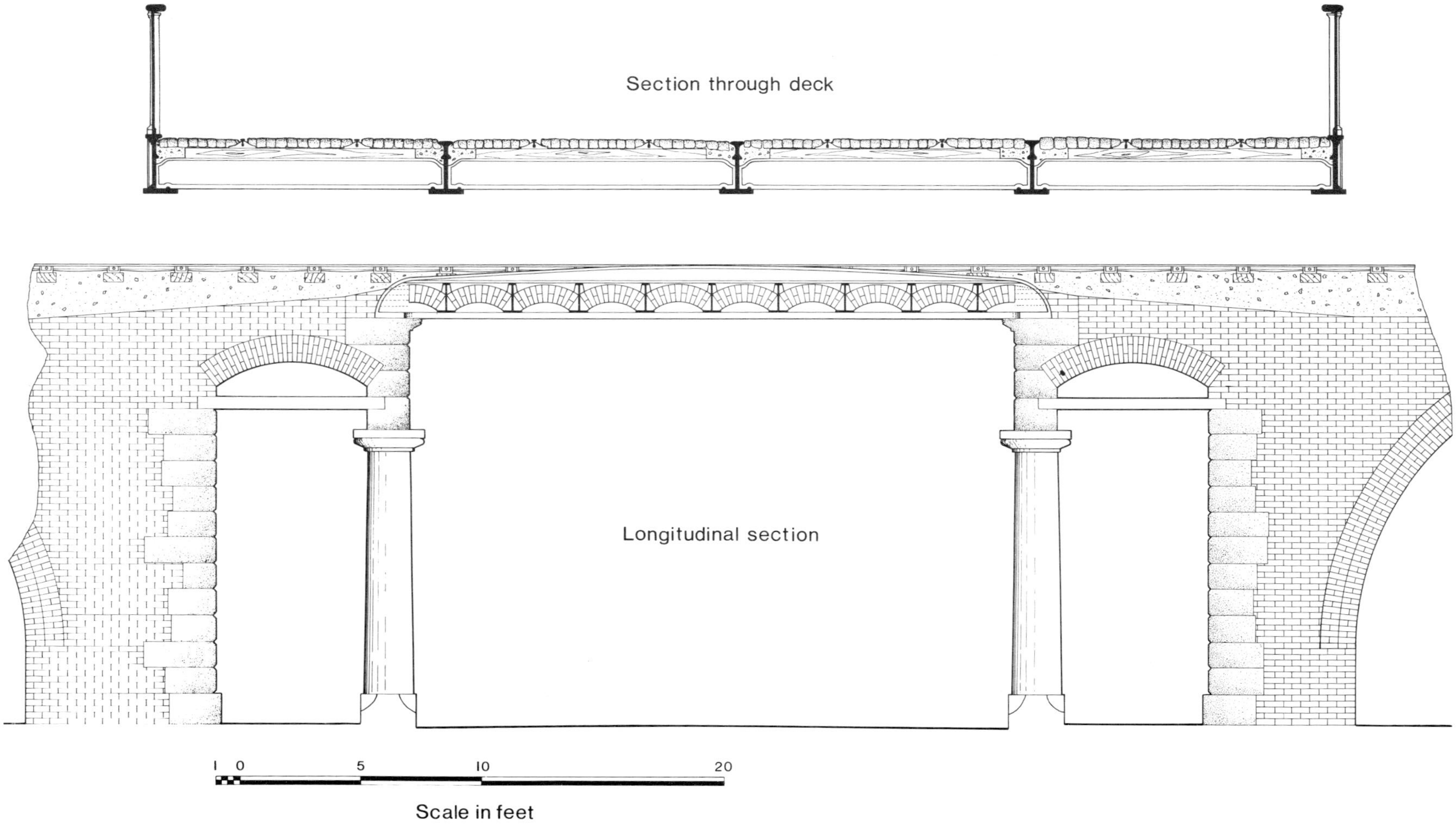

Section through deck

Longitudinal section

Scale in feet

20

10

5

0

The Water Street Bridge: sections.

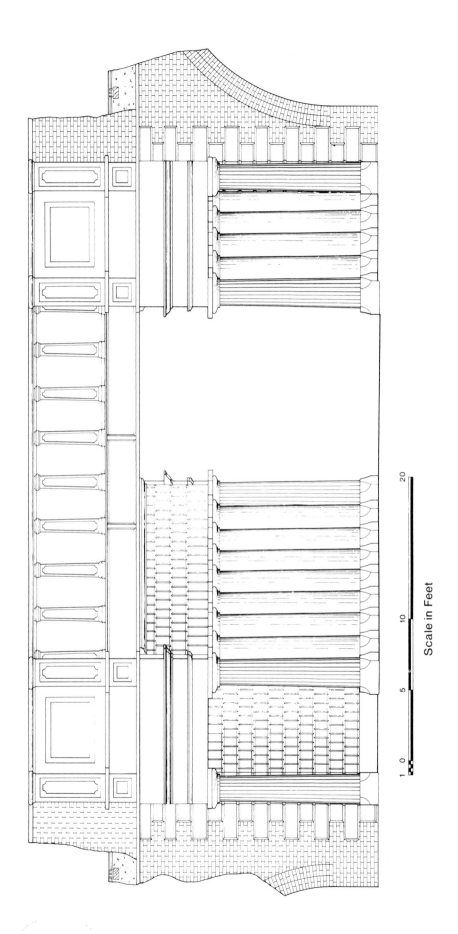

Scale in Feet

The Water Street Bridge: elevation.

The latter sprang from the footpath side of the entablature, and the necessary reactions may be assumed to have been generated within the entablature. It is possible that the ceiling contained tie-bars. The abutment piers were of brick, but illustrations show a rusticated finish to the footpath side which may have been either masonry or stucco. A cast-iron parapet rose from rail level. The junction between the sections of the parapet were concealed by fluted pilaster strips. This format was repeated in the parapets over the footways.

Notes

[1] A. F. Sealy and D. W. Walters, 'The first railway architect', *Architectural Review*, May 1964.

[2] W. O. Skeat, *George Stephenson the Engineer and his Letters*, Institute of Mechanical Engineers, 1973.

[3] Thomas Summerside, *Anecdotes, Reminiscenses and Conversations of and with the late George Stephenson*, 1878.

[4] *George and Robert Stephenson*, p. 92.

[5] *Life of George Stephenson*, pp. 49–50.

[6] MS Autobiography of T. L. Gooch, Library of the Institute of Civil Engineers.

[7] Deed of Indentures of Apprenticeship between T. L. Gooch and George Stephenson, Library of the Institute of Mechanical Engineers.

[8] Diaries of T. L. Gooch, Library of the Institute of Civil Engineers.

[9] Smiles, *Life of George Stephenson*, p. 441.

[10] Letter to Thomas Telford from James Mills, who inspected the line on behalf of Telford and the Exchequer Loan Commissioners, 15 December 1828, Library of the Institute of Civil Engineers, T/LM/14.

[11] A. W. Skempton, *William Chapman (1749–1832), Civil Engineer*, Transactions of the Newcomen Society, vol. 46, 1973–74, p. 50.

[12] Rees, *Cyclopedia*, 1813, vol. 25, article on oblique arches.

[13] Peter Nicholson, *A Popular and Practical Treatise on Masonry and Stone Cutting*, 1827.

[14] List of bridges to be completed, compiled by T. L. Gooch for Thomas Telford, Library of the Institute of Civil Engineers.

[15] Rolt, *George and Robert Stephenson*, p. 248, quoting from F. R. Condor, *Personal Recollections of English Engineers of the Railway System in the United Kingdom*, 1868.

[16] Committee on the Liverpool and Manchester Railroad, *Proceedings of the Committee of the House of Commons on the Liverpool and Manchester Railroad Bill*, 1825, Maps, Plans and Sections attached.

[17] Agreement for the Irwell Bridge, 2 February 1829, Manchester Public Library, Archives Department.

[18] 10 Geo. IV, cap. 35, 14 May 1829.

[19] Minutes of the Board of Directors, 19 January 1829.

[20] Letter from James Mills to Thomas Telford, 13 December 1828, Library of the Institute of Civil Engineers, T/LM/14.

[21] *Manchester Guardian*, 23 May 1829.

[22] Minutes of the Board of Directors, 19 January 1829.

[23] Pigot and Dean, *A New Directory of Manchester and Salford*, 1821–22.

[24] *The Engineer*, 25 March 1881.

[25] Minutes of the Board of Directors, 29 June 1829.

[26] *Manchester Guardian*, 17 April 1830.

[27] *Ibid.*, 1 May 1830.

[28] *Ibid.*, 15 May 1830.

[29] Minutes of the Finance Committee, 20 April 1831.

[30] Minutes of the Board of Directors, 19 July 1830.

[31] *Manchester Guardian*, 28 August 1830.

[32] Minutes of the Board of Directors, 2 March 1829.

[33] *Ibid.*, 16 March 1829.

[34] *The North Eastern Railway*, p. 93; A. W. Sealy and D. W. Walters, 'The first iron railway bridge', *Architectural Review*, March 1963.

[35] Eaton Hodgkinson, 'Theoretical and experimental researches to ascertain the strength and best form for the iron beams', *Transactions of the Manchester Literary and Philosophical Society*, 2 April 1830.

[36] Minutes of the Board of Directors, 7 December 1829.

[37] *Ibid.*, 12 April 1830.

[38] *Manchester City News*, 26 November 1904.

[39] Francis Wishaw, *Railways of Great Britain and Ireland*, 1842, rpr. David and Charles, 1970, p. 199.

[40] *Manchester Guardian*, 15 March 1830.

[41] William Fairbairn, *The Use of Cast and Wrought Iron for Building Purposes*, 1857, p. 24.

[42] Hodgkinson, *op. cit.*

[43] These drawings are now in the possession of the Chief Civil Engineer's Office, British Railways, to whom I am grateful for assistance.

Chapter IV

The warehouse and station

To a large extent the provision of depot facilities depended upon the organisation of the carrying department. In its coverage of this aspect of the Railway Company's activities the 1826 Act had been modelled upon the circumstances prevailing in Manchester with regard to existing carriers. All three navigation companies in addition to taking tolls for the use of their waterways were empowered to act as carriers. It was therefore in the interests of equity that the Railway Company should receive similar powers. The exercise of these powers, however, was left to the Company's discretion.

Two courses of action lay open. First, the Company could confine its role to the receipt of tolls and contract out the carrying powers as the Stockton and Darlington Railway did.[1] The situation facing the Liverpool and Manchester, however, was not entirely comparable. The latter was fundamentally a coal carrier, and whilst coal did figure in the traffic prospects of the Liverpool and Manchester Railway it was not accorded a central role, greater emphasis being laid on the carriage of merchandise and passengers. Thus, whereas the Stockton line had only to provide coal staithes, the Liverpool and Manchester Railway needed more comprehensive facilities. The directors had to consider upon whom the responsibility for constructing them might fall.[2] If the Railway Company did not act as carrier it was possible that a major outlay on warehouses and stock could be saved. Secondly, the Company could invest in the provision of carrying facilities. As was apparent from the events of 1825, carrying and warehousing played a large part in the profitability of the navigation companies. The Mersey and Irwell Navigation particularly benefited from its virtual monopoly of warehouse space on the banks of the Irwell. In the event the second viewpoint prevailed.[3] As the construction of the line was consuming all existing funds, Moss proposed a fresh capital issue of £127,000 to finance the carrying department. Accordingly a clause was inserted to that effect in the 1829 Bill.

The acquisition of additional powers occupied twelve months, and not until June 1829 did the board again turn its attention to the carrying department.[4] At first it seemed that the Railway Company had opted to act as carrier, for on 29 June the board resolved that the Company should convey on its own behalf without the intervention of a separate carrier, though not to the exclusion of outsiders. It transpired that its intentions were less definite. By September the possibility of contracting the passenger side to Lacy, a Manchester coach proprietor, was being investigated.[5] In the same month negotiations started with the New Quay Company with a view to their acting as carriers on the railway.[6] Formed in 1823 as an independent carrier on the Mersey and Irwell Navigation, the firm operated eighteen vessels and dealt exclusively in merchandise. Its success had been limited by the Navigation Company's warehouse monopoly, and this probably motivated its interest in the Railway. After discussions the New Quay Company proposed terms.[7] The Liverpool and Manchester Railway was to find wagons and motive power to operate the line for the hire of which the New Quay was to pay rent. Additionally, the Railway Company should receive £150 to £200 per annum as rent for a store at Liverpool. As the New Quay Company already had warehouses in Water Street, it felt that only a shed would be required at Manchester, for which £50 to £100 was considered appropriate. These terms were approved by the Railway and the preparation of contracts followed.[8] At the eleventh hour the New Quay Company declined to ratify the terms and the proposals collapsed. This prompted the Railway Company to instruct the committee for planning the depots to take into consideration the possibility of the Railway Company itself acting as a carrier of merchandise between Liverpool and Manchester.[9]

The situation by this time was beginning to assume some urgency. The acquisition of land in Manchester, the passage of the 1829 Act and the negotiations with the New Quay Company had taken three years. Elsewhere the rest of the line was nearing completion. In November the management of the Company was reorganised. New committees were formed to deal with the altered conditions that would arise from operation rather than construction.[10] The No. 2 Committee was constituted to plan the building of warehouses and offices. Its composition reflected its duties. The chairman, John Moss, was also deputy chairman of the Company; his business interests included timber, sugar plantations, oil mills and privateering, all of which served to support the firm of Moss Rogers and Moss, by the 1820s Liverpool's leading bank.[11] Robert Benson, with Moss, was one of the earliest subscribers to the Railway and had joined the board in 1826. He was partner to James Cropper, a fellow director of the Railway, in the firm of Cropper Benson, Liverpool cotton merchants.[12] The remaining two members, Charles Tayleur and James Bourne, both had mercantile backgrounds. Tayleur had joined the board in 1829 to replace Lister Ellis. He was one of the initial subscribers to the Railway and a leading shareholder by 1829. Bourne was involved in coal mining, with pits in the Sutton area between Manchester and Liverpool.

All had useful experience in local commerce, but there is little indication that any of them had previous experience in the organisation of a transport undertaking comparable to the Liverpool and Manchester Railway. It seems probable, therefore, that their actions were to a large extent to be governed by observations of the way rival transport concerns approached similar problems. As in several respects the Liverpool and Manchester Railway was by nature closer to the waterways than to existing railways, particularly with regard to its traffic prospects, it is reasonable to suggest that the committee was inclined to adapt the experience of the waterways to its own situation. This approach is exemplified by the construction of the Railway Company's Manchester warehouse.

A hundred and fifty years later it is impossible to gain more than a superficial impression of the material upon which the committee could have formulated its ideas. Few warehouses of the period survive, and the remaining examples are not necessarily representative. Thus any review of warehouse development based upon surviving examples must be in part speculative.

Although numerically preponderant, the urban warehouses of the mercantile trades were less important in the history of design. It was within the canal and dock basins that the most dynamic developments occurred, encouraged by open sites and corporate capital. By 1820 the structural identity of the warehouse had attained some degree of uniformity in these areas.

The principal load-bearing function was performed by brick or masonry walls and an internal timber frame. Most commonly the latter consisted of floorboards, bridging joists of 4 in. × 6 in. or 6 in. × 8 in. section supported by main beams of rectangular or square section. When main spans exceeded 13 ft. or 14 ft. it was usual to provide intermediate support by vertical timber posts in single rows or grid formation for larger areas. Either the storey-posts supported individual transverse beams or, alternatively, a line of storey-posts carried a single beam, extending the length of the building, upon which transverse beams rested. The latter allowed a wider column interval, with increased unobstructed floor space. In both cases the beams were usually continuous over the posts and the superincumbent load of the posts was transmitted through the fibres of the beams. This occasioned a punching shear effect which in extreme cases might cause crushing, and consequent transverse failure of the floor beams. To obviate this risk, caps were interposed between the storey-posts and the horizontal beams to distribute the load over a wider area.

The Pease Warehouse, Hull, built in 1742, possibly the earliest standing warehouse in Britain: *(above left)* the gable frontage dates from 1880; *(above right)* the internal spine wall. The vertical timber posts are a later edition.

London Dock North Quay warehouse stacks 1–5 *(right)*: interior, showing storey-posts and the internal load-bearing walls, which divide the interior into four units.

East India Company Cutler Street Warehouse *(below left)*: cruciform section cast-iron columns. *Greater London Council Photographic Unit*

Rochdale Canal Company warehouse at Sowerby Bridge *(below right)*. Vertical cast-iron columns of hollow cylindrical cross-section support transverse timber ribs upon which rest secondary beams. These in turn carry the bridging joists and the floorboards.

The Old Quay Company's New Botany Warehouse, Manchester, dating from 1824. *(Below)* ground-floor cast-iron columns. The slenderness ratio is mature but the wooden caps are a 'hang-over' from earlier timber storey-posts. *(Above right)* timber storey-posts. *(Below right)* base of the ground-floor cast-iron columns. The concave cup accommodates the base of the column and allows movement to compensate for settlement, which would otherwise fracture the iron column.

Occasionally, internal load-bearing walls are to be found. At the Pease Warehouse, Hull, of 1742, a spinal wall extends the length of the principal axis, dividing the building longitudinally into two halves. This rises to third-floor level and supports the floor joists at each level. A similar system was employed in warehouse stacks 1–5 at London Dock, where the spine wall was supplemented by a transverse wall dividing the interior into four units.

The development of fire-resisting structures in other areas of building, notably in textile mills, attained only limited popularity in warehouses before the introduction of wrought-iron beams. Cast-iron beams were less well suited to the concentrated floor loadings of warehouses. The most widespread concession to fire control entailed enclosing the staircases in masonry or brick towers, thus isolating the stairs and creating a safe exit from a burning building. Stair towers also inhibited the spread of fire between floors.

The use of cast iron was generally confined to vertical

supports. In London the earliest surviving examples of cast-iron columns until recently appeared to be those included in the fabric of the South Quay stacks, London Dock, dating from 1810. By 1820 similar cruciform-section columns had appeared in the 1820 extension of the East India Company's Cutler Street Warehouse. The cruciform cross-section was the earliest form of cast-iron column used in building. In London it remained popular throughout the nineteenth century, but elsewhere it was supplanted by the hollow cylindrical cross-section, with its higher moment of inertia. Early nineteenth-century examples with characteristically high slenderness ratios remain on the Calder Navigation at Wakefield and Sowerby Bridge.

The structural characteristics of the Manchester canal warehouses followed these general patterns, although the introduction of cast-iron columns was somewhat delayed. The largest survival from the 1820s is the New Botany Warehouse, built in 1824 by the Old Quay Company. On all but the ground floor, timber posts are used for vertical support. The cast-iron columns of the ground floor are of hollow cylindrical section with a mature slenderness ratio. To accommodate structural settlement the columns have bases machined to the convex segment of a sphere which is accommodated in a cup cast into the baseplate. The fact that the cast-iron columns are con-

fined to the ground floor is probably due to the riverside location of the building. Should the river flood and water accumulate for any length of time, timber would be vulnerable to decay but cast iron would be unaffected. The only surviving building of the 1820s to employ cast-iron columns throughout is the Rochdale Canal Company's warehouse at Dale Street, but the origins of this building are peculiar.[13]

Although in the main structurally conventional, a number of Manchester warehouses seem to have displayed a more innovatory approach to the question of layout. Two distinctive developments have been identified.[14] The first appears in the 1740 Rock House Warehouse, and was prompted by the site characteristics prevailing on the banks of the Irwell. The Manchester bank consists mainly of a vertical sandstone face of varying height. The Rock House Warehouse faced on to the river and boats moored alongside discharged by jib cranes through loopholes. The ground floor of the building was at river level but the road level to the rear of the building was 20 ft. higher. Transit through the warehouse thus involved movement between floors.

The second significant development took place at the Castlefield Basin of the Bridgewater Canal and was in evidence until recently in the Grocers' Company Warehouse of 1770–80.[15] The structural form of the building was conventional, with external brick load-bearing walls and an internal spine wall supporting transverse timber beams. Its innovation lay in the ground plan, which embodied internal transhipment facilities. An arm of the canal passed through shipping doors in the façade, allowing boats to enter the building. Goods were loaded either direct on to the ground floor or through hatches positioned above the dock in the floors above. By 1793 the building had been extended and, whilst the new addition did not include internal loading facilities, it embodied an improved structural layout. The spine wall was replaced by a series of transverse walls running from front to back. The building was thus divided into compartments. The floor joists extended between the transverse walls. This plan gave uninterrupted communication from the front to the rear of the building. Again, the nature of the site dictated that the road level to the rear should correspond with the second floor level.

The Grocers' Company Warehouse was destroyed in 1960, but a similar building remains in the same locality: the Merchants' Warehouse. Internally this building is divided by transverse brick walls at 23 ft. intervals, which carry 12 in. × 8 in. timber floor beams. The two central divisions enclose wet docks from which unloading took

Rochdale Canal Company warehouse at Dale Street, Manchester. This warehouse is believed to have previously been sited in Yorkshire. The diagonal braces may be unique.

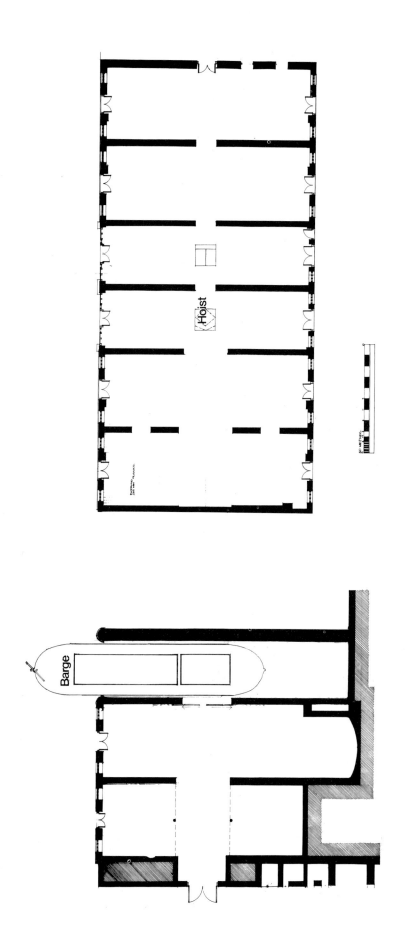

The Merchants' Warehouse, Bridgewater Canal, Castlefield basin. (*Left*) the internal loading dock; (*right*) plan across the ground floor. Note particularly the transverse walls which support the floor joists.

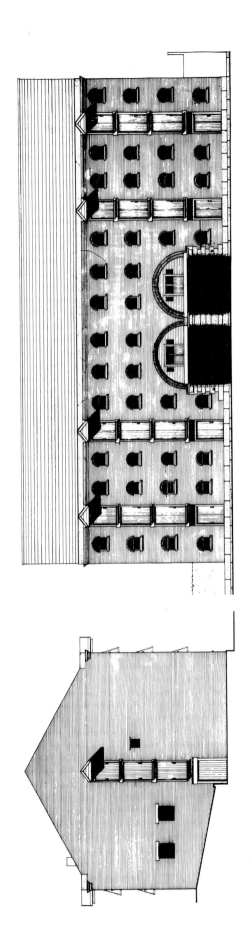

40 METRES

The Merchants' Warehouse: elevation.

The Merchants' Company Warehouse, Manchester. *(Above)* the canalside elevation with the internal loading facilities in the centre flanked by vertical loading bays or 'loopholes'. *(Below)* interior. The internal walls divide the building into units and the floor joists are supported by these walls.

place vertically through traps in the floors above. The internal loading bays are supplemented by loopholes in the façade facing on to the canal proper. The rear façade contains further loopholes which give access from each floor into the street.

These design features attained widespread popularity. By 1800 the ideas had been used by the Bridgewater Canal Company in Manchester and Liverpool, whilst both the Rochdale and Leeds to Liverpool canals had adapted the design to their own needs.

It is not clear who was responsible for turning the carrying committee's ideas into working designs. Possibly the Company drawing office at Clayton Square, Liverpool, carried out the work. There, until November 1829, Thomas Gooch was chief and possibly sole draughtsman, after which date he replaced Joseph Locke as resident on the western end of the line.[16] As his new post is unlikely to have permitted him to continue work in the office, the warehouse designs would need to have been prepared between July 1829, when the site plans were drawn up, and November. As personal secretary to Stephenson Gooch was replaced by Frederick Swanwick, but it is nowhere stated that Swanwick took over Gooch's duties as draughtsman.

The Company records omit any direct reference to the warehouse designer, and no other source has been found to throw light on the matter. Only one entry in the board minutes might provide a clue. On 17 May 1830,[17] whilst the buildings were under construction, a Mr Haigh was requested to appoint a competent person to oversee the works. Thomas Haigh was a Liverpool architect and surveyor.[18] The design of much of the subsequent building work for the railway can be definitively attributed to him, and when the warehouse accommodation at Manchester was extended in 1831 Haigh produced the designs.[19]

At the general meeting of March 1830 the Company announced that it had projected warehousing for 10,000 bales of cotton or other merchandise in proportion.[20] At the end of the month the *Manchester Guardian*[21] carried a notice to builders inviting tenders for the construction of five warehouses to be built of brick. The bricks were to be found by the Company and were probably part of the consignment which George Jones of Salford had delivered during December.[22] This was the largest quantity of bricks ordered by the Company over the period of the construction of the line and must in part have been intended for the building of the viaduct in addition to the station and the warehouses. The successful contractor was to be responsible for obtaining the rest of the materials, and security of £1,000 was required.

By 19 April the tenders were in.[23] Five firms submitted estimates: J. B. Brockbank and Samuel Ward and Sons of Manchester proposed £12,000; David Bellhouse, Jnr, £12,250; James White, £12,683; William Southern, £13,989; and Bartin Haigh of Liverpool, £14,000. Only the first two were considered, but there were reservations about Brockbank and his partner. Brockbank was, of course, the contractor for the Irwell Bridge with Alexander Fyfe. His association with Ward on this occasion probably reflects the different nature of the contract. The board required testimonials for Ward but, whether these proved unsatisfactory or whether the events at the Irwell Bridge were the cause, Brockbank failed to qualify. The tender was let instead to David Bellhouse on the under-standing that two of the warehouses were to be finished by 31 July and the remainder by 15 August.[24]

The Bellhouses with their ramified family connections occupy a central place in the nineteenth-century building

Liverpool Road, the warehouse: *(above left)* south or rail eleva-tion. The three rail entrances alternate with conventional load-ing bays. *(Above right)* north elevation, showing discharging and loading doors and former access to the rail bridge link with the later warehouse No. 2. *(Below left)* ground-floor level. The timber storey-posts to the right carried the support for the internal rail tracks. After the rails were removed, about 1860, the floor levels were adjusted to eliminate the loading docks. The vertical supports for the new level consist of re-used sleep-ers. *(Below right)* rail support and storey-posts in the eastern-most bay. The redundant sleepers used to readjust the floor levels above, following the removal of the tracks, can be clearly seen.

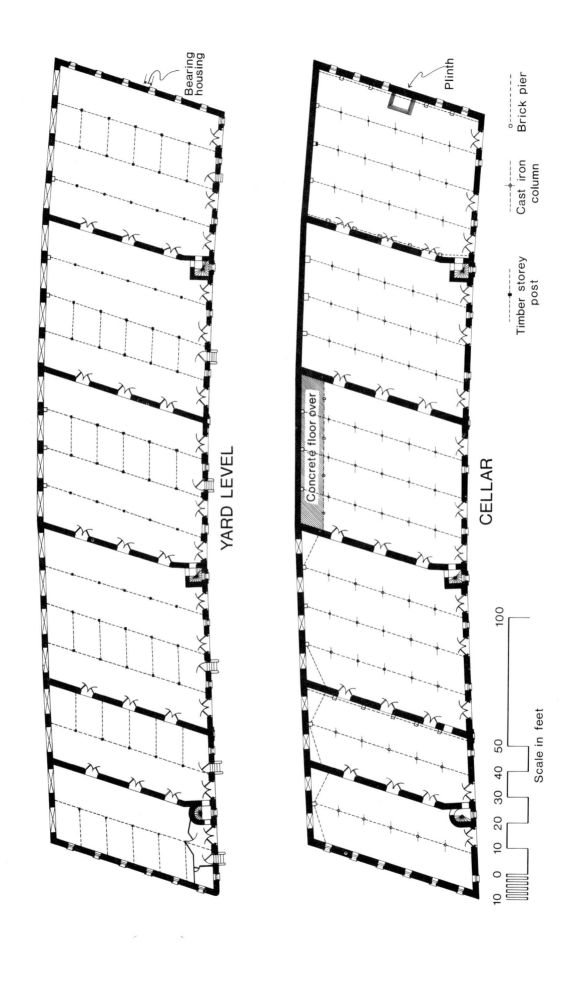

YARD LEVEL

CELLAR

Bearing housing

Plinth

Concrete floor over

Brick pier

Cast iron column

Timber storey post

Scale in feet

10 0 10 20 30 40 50 100

Liverpool Road Station warehouse: floor and reflected beam plans, 1978.

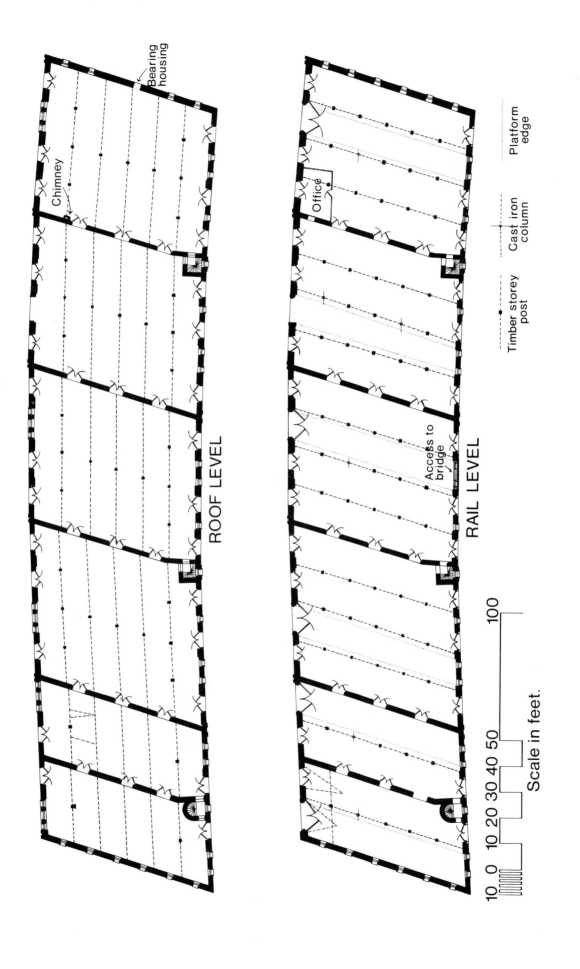

Bearing housing

Chimney

ROOF LEVEL

Office

Access to bridge

RAIL LEVEL

— — — Timber storey post

———+——— Cast iron column

.... Platform edge

Scale in feet.

10 0   10 20 30 40 50   100

Liverpool Road Station warehouse: floor and reflected beam plans, 1978.

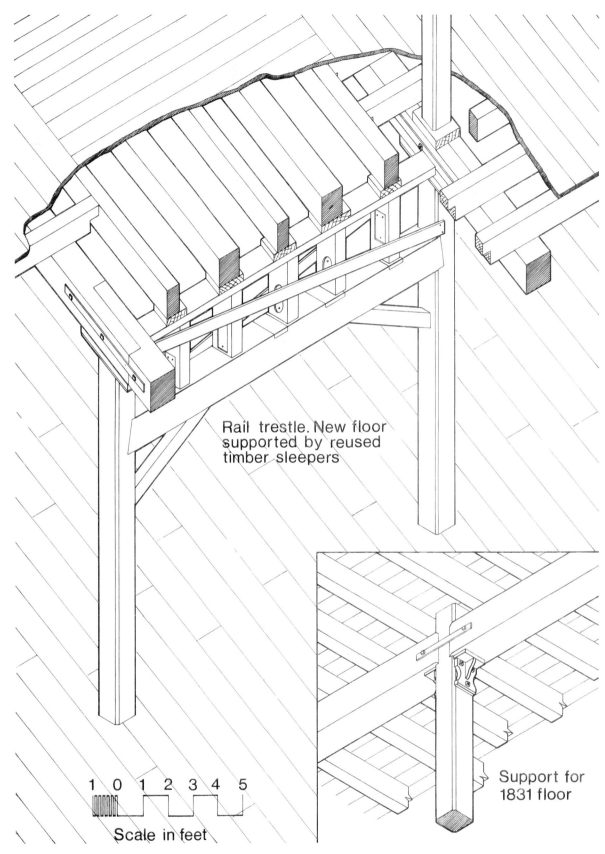

Rail trestle. New floor
supported by reused
timber sleepers

Support for
1831 floor

1 0 1 2 3 4 5

Scale in feet

Liverpool Road Station warehouse: the present floor structures, ground-floor level.

RAIL LEVEL

CELLAR

Mouldings
at x

See p. 44

Scale in feet

1
0
1
2
3
4
5

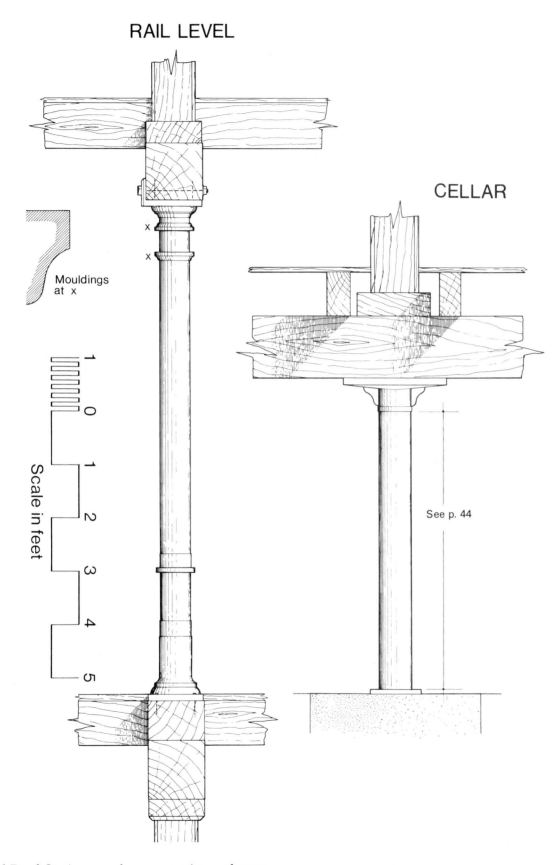

Liverpool Road Station warehouse: cast-iron columns.

history of Manchester. At the end of the eighteenth century the brothers David and George had been joiners and carpenters.[25] The former was probably the father of David Bellhouse Jnr. By the mid-1820s the firm of David Bellhouse and Son had grown to become the town's leading timber importer, with powered sawmills adjoining the Old Quay. In 1824 it had begun to transport its timber from Liverpool by means of a steam tug hauling specialised lighters.[26] One of the Bellhouses owned a brickfield in the Castlefield area, and a later trade directory indicated that by 1840 the building firm of David Bellhouse was operating independently.[27]

The construction of the warehouses was relatively uneventful, although in May 1830[28] it was felt advisable to call upon Haigh to appoint a competent person to remain on the spot to superintend the brickwork and masonry. Progress was rapid, for by 24 July 1830 the *Manchester Guardian*[29] could report that the warehouses were nearing completion and that the whole range was roofed over. It was sufficiently complete by the opening day to act as a reception area for the guests who did finally reach Manchester. The upper storey had been given over to a '. . . cold collation provided by Mr. Lymm of the Waterloo Hotel . . .'[30] which was intended to be consumed by a thousand people. Bellhouse had constructed a temporary timber staircase to give access to the upper storeys. In the event it was a sombre and dispirited affair, marred by Huskisson's unfortunate accident with the *Rocket* and the hostile mob which awaited Wellington at the Manchester end. Of course it rained.

The building as it stands today is a remarkable survival. With the exception of the intermediate floor, installed later in the western end, it is virtually unaltered. The ground plan consists of five major transverse divisions, the easternmost of which is subdivided into two equal halves. Prior to alterations of 1831 the floor levels comprised cellar, ground floor at street level, rail level and top storey. The linear axis of the building conforms to the curvature of the railway viaduct. The north elevation rises from street level, but the south façade is orientated to the rail level of the viaduct. Transit through the warehouse involves movement between levels. At rail level the façade is pierced by double loading doors and loopholes, the latter of which rise to the top storey. In 1830 there were six sets of double doors corresponding to the internal divisions and fourteen loopholes, three for each full division, and one each for the easternmost two. The double doors led from the viaduct into the building, and, by means of a timber trestle incorporated into the internal structure, rail tracks passed from the exterior into the building. Inside, the rails were flanked by wharves which allowed wagons to be unloaded direct. To the rear or street side of the building loopholes served to discharge goods on to carts and to receive new loads.

The debt the design owes to the Manchester warehouses described previously will be immediately evident. The division of the building into separate compartments has its parallel in the 1793 extension to the Grocers' Company warehouses and the Merchants' Warehouse. Equally, the transhipment facilities have their origins in the earlier canal warehouses, with their internal docks. Finally, the operation of the warehouse on split levels is a clear adaptation of the tradition established by the Rock House Warehouse and its successors.

Of the structural characteristics of the warehouse, the most obvious feature is the similarity between its system of vertical supports and that of near-by canal warehouses. The principal floor beams extend from the front wall to the back and consist of 13 in. square section deal baulks. At intervals these are scarfed by half lap joints secured by wrought-iron straps. The bridging joists which support 2 in. floor boards are of 5 in. $\times$ 10 in. section and run from the transverse walls longitudinally over the main beams. The main beams are supported at 10 ft. intervals by timber storey-posts, the free-standing height of which is 9 ft. on the upper two floors and 13 ft. at ground-floor level. The cross-sections are respectively 9½ in. $\times$ 9½ in., 10 in. $\times$ 10 in. and 11 in. $\times$ 11 in. At rail level the storey-posts carried the additional load of the railway into the building by means of horizontal beams spanning between two rows of posts in the four major divisions, and between a single row of posts and the walls at the eastern end. Diagonal braces reduce the free span. At cellar level the timber posts give way to cast-iron columns of cylindrical cross-section with a mean diameter of 7⅝ in. Their free-standing height varies between 5 ft. 6 in. at the western end and 8 ft. 6 in. at the eastern end to maintain the ground floor at street level. This combined use of timber and cast iron for the vertical supports has previously been described as applied to the Old Quay Company's New Botany Warehouse of 1824. A similar flood risk prevailed on the Railway Company's site.

The roof is of conventional form for the period. Two queen-post trusses share a common tie-beam which extends between the transverse walls and is supported intermediately by timber storey-posts. The central post carries the valley plate and gutters. At the front and rear of the building a platform extends from the wall to the first line of posts. Upon this are mounted the crane winches. The cranes are of a type common in the early

nineteenth century. A winch barrel mounted between two cast-iron pedestals has attached to it two contra-wound ropes. As one rope unwinds, the other is wound on. To operate the hoist, a load must descend to balance the ascending load. Control of the descent is by means of a brake wheel checked by a system of levers and ropes operable from each floor level.

The architectural treatment of the building is restrained. The only concessions to decoration are the use of divided pilaster strips to denote the internal divisions, and the use of stone for the quoins around the shipping doors, for the lintels and sills of the windows, and for the cornice copings and lunettes. Interestingly, the profile of the cornice moulding and the distinctive style of the quoins are repeated on the Patricroft Bridge over the Bridgewater Canal.

It remains briefly to chronicle the alterations which affected the warehouse in subsequent years, the most important of which occurred in the year following its completion. Towards the end of January 1831[31] it was decided to install an intermediate floor between rail level and the ground floor of the three western divisions. This was possible because of the 14 ft. headroom available, but it entailed the loss of rail access to the affected areas. The new floor was supported by the transverse walls and by cast-iron brackets attached to the storey-posts.

At the end of 1830 Stephenson was instructed to prepare plans for mechanising the lifting gear.[32] In the fol-

Liverpool Road, warehouse: *(above)* cellar, showing cast-iron columns; *(middle)* roof trusses and supports 'or valley plate; *(below)* roof truss in easternmost bay. The crane platform and the stair tower are also visible.

Liverpool Road, warehouse: crane winch. The contra-wound ropes are in place. To the right of the picture is the brake drum, and to the left the cog for the powered drive. The belt drum is a later addition.

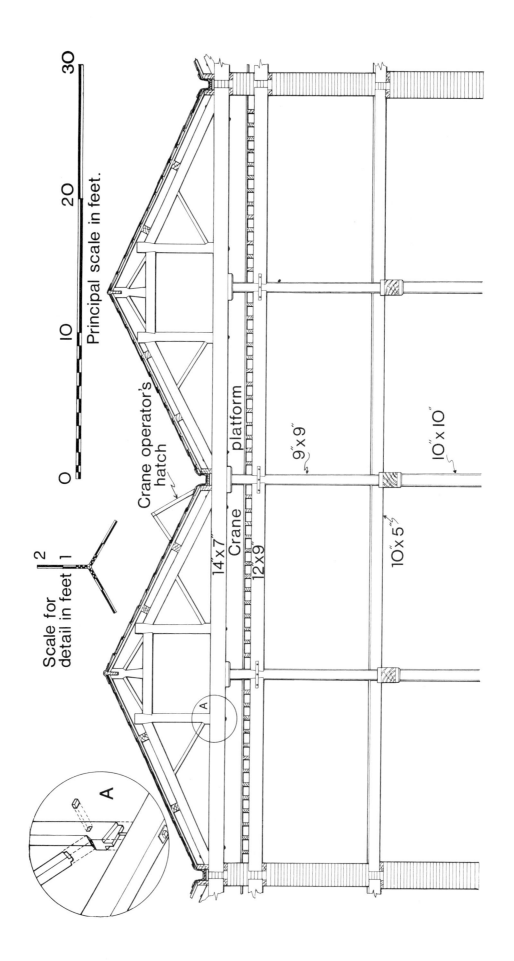

30

20

Principal scale in feet.

10

0

Crane operator's hatch

Scale for detail in feet

2

1

14"x7"

Crane platform

12"x9"

9"x9"

10"x10"

10"x5"

A

A

Liverpool Road Station warehouse: section through top floor and roof trusses.

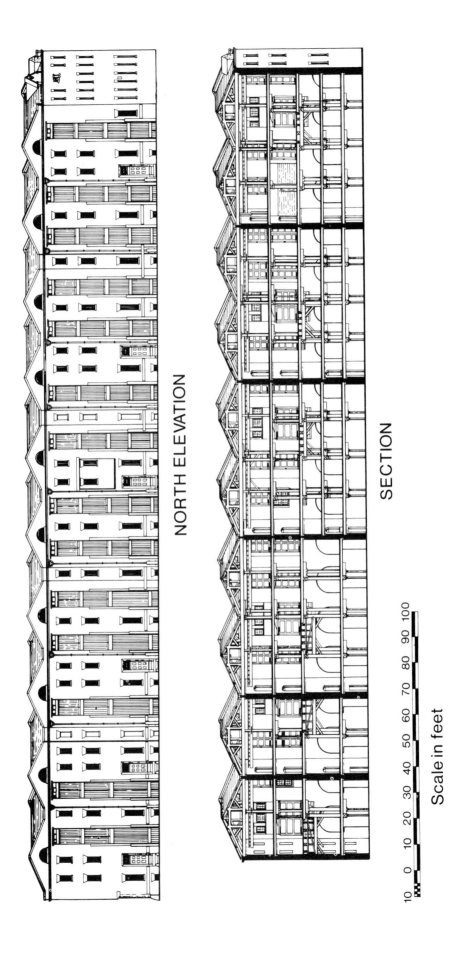

NORTH ELEVATION

SECTION

Scale in feet

10 0 10 20 30 40 50 60 70 80 90 100

Liverpool Road Station warehouse: north elevation and section.

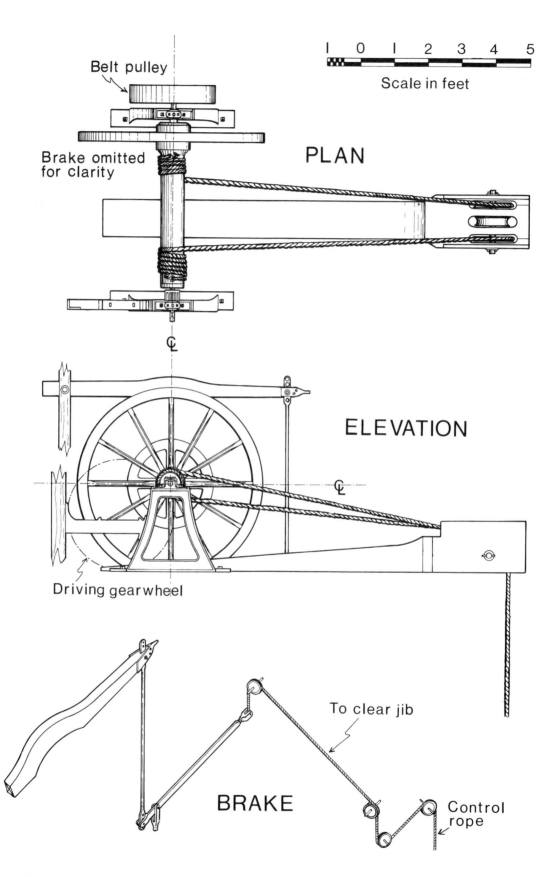

Belt pulley

Brake omitted for clarity

PLAN

Scale in feet

CL

ELEVATION

CL

Driving gearwheel

To clear jib

BRAKE

Control rope

Liverpool Road Station warehouse: crane.

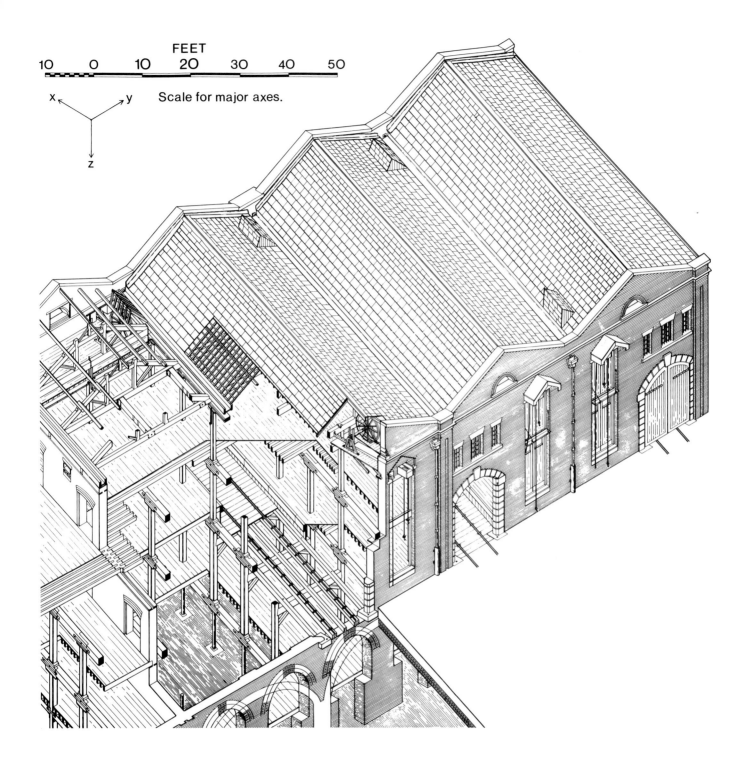

FEET

10   0   10   20   30   40   50

x ↙ ↘ y   Scale for major axes.

z ↓

Liverpool Road Station warehouse: reconstruction of south elevation and section *c.* 1835.

Liverpool Road, warehouse: *(above)* main rail access doors and *(below)* support for the additional floor of 1831.

lowing May Thompson Swift and Cole, of Bolton, secured the contract to provide a steam engine for £340. The boiler and steam mains were apparently to be built in the company workshops. The new engine was accommodated at the western end of the building. The boilers were adjacent to the engine house, and a tall chimney was built to dispel the smoke. The power was transmitted from the flywheel into the warehouse by shafting and vertically to the top floor by an upright shaft, supported at cellar level by a brick plinth. Across the top floor the line shafting was attached to timber beams mounted between the roof trusses. Where the shafting interrupted the transverse walls, bearing boxes were installed, and because of the angularity of the building it was necessary to block several doorways that lay in the path of the shafting. The final drive to the jiggers was less obvious at the time of the survey in 1978. A geared drive was evident at the end of the winch barrel but the intermediate motion between the line shafting and the jigger had disappeared without trace. Most probably it consisted of a belt drive with provisions for reversing. The drives were progressively extended to each section of the warehouse, but not until 1835 was the job completed.

One development which has left no trace was the installation of a wrought-iron water tank in the top room of the easternmost division. Its purpose was fire prevention, and, according to the *Manchester Guardian*,[33] its capacity was 12,000 gallons, or about 1,927 cu. ft. The contract was let to Michael Woods for £152. That such an enormous vessel should have left no visible sign is particularly surprising.

By 1831 the expansion of freight traffic was overtaking the ability of the single warehouse to cope. The pressure was increased by the Bolton and Leigh Railway's traffic, which had to be accommodated within the eastern end of the building.[34] In January Haigh Franklin of Liverpool were requested to prepare designs for a new shipping shed to be erected at the south-eastern corner of the site and for a further range of warehouses capable of holding 10,000 bags of cotton. Five Manchester firms tendered for the work. The two highest quotations were from William Southern and David Bellhouse at £15,299 and £15,055 respectively. The choice lay between James White at £13,900 and Samuel Buxton's £13,885. The latter was successful.[35] During the course of construction Mr Earle (one of the directors) recommended that a third floor be added to the original two, and for £4,675 Buxton agreed to include it in his contract. When Wishaw inspected the site in 1839[36] he described the additional buildings as consisting of two warehouses: one, 200 ft. × 70 ft., parallel to the 1830 stack and 60 ft. to the rear; the other, 200 ft. × 90 ft., at right-angles to the original stack and 75 ft. away.

The south gable of No. 3 stack abutted the viaduct, and in order to allow covered unloading three tracks ran into the building from rail level. No. 2 was isolated from the railway, so that, in order to secure covered unloading facilities for this building, turntables were installed in No. 3 and a covered bridge was built between Nos. 2 and 3 which carried tracks across into No. 2. The bridge eventually formed a bottleneck, preventing wagons regaining the viaduct when the roads in No. 3 were obstructed. In 1838 a bridge was constructed from the south face of No. 2 into No. 1, permitting wagons to follow a circular course back on to the viaduct.[37] Warehouses 2 and 3 were demolished in the early 1860s to make way for the L.N.W.R.[38] extension, but evidence of the bridge connection into No. 1 remains in the north face of the warehouse.

It is less easy to identify the origins of the design for the station, as passenger carriers prior to the Liverpool and Manchester Railway operated under different circumstances. The majority of travellers went by road, either

The warehouses at Wapping, Liverpool. Unloading took place from the wagons through traps in the warehouse floors.

using their own personal transport or by stage wagons, coaches or omnibus. Commercial schedules were oriented around established hotels and inns, which, in addition to providing refreshments and accommodation, acted as agents for the carriers, selling tickets and servicing the vehicles.

Canal companies also handled a considerable volume of passenger traffic. In Manchester, both the Bridgewater and the Mersey and Irwell had secured a share of the trade. The Bridgewater packet boats began operating in 1767 with a daily service between Manchester and Altrincham in both directions. The Mersey and Irwell followed later, starting a service in 1806 between Manchester and Runcorn, with a connecting steamer continuing on to Liverpool. Each company provided accommodation at the boarding and landing points. The Bridgewater had a ticket office and waiting room at the Castlefields basin, adjacent to the Grocers' Company Warehouse, whilst the Old Quay Company packet wharf was on the Salford side of the river, with a pier below the New Bailey Bridge and a waiting room beneath the roadway.[39]

Earlier railways had had only a limited involvement with passengers. The South Wales lines were active carriers, but the degree to which this was official policy is uncertain.[40] The first passengers on the Stockton and Darlington Railway had been carried on an informal basis, but in October 1825 the company applied for a passenger licence, and from the 10th of the month a service between the two towns was conducted by the company itself. In April 1826 Richard Pickersgill, a carrier on the Great North Road, contracted for the whole of the trade, an arrangement which was short-lived, for the following month the contract was revoked and the line thrown open on payment of a toll. Not until 1833 did the company undertake to provide terminal facilities when a small goods warehouse was converted into a booking office and waiting room at North Road, Darlington.[41]

To some extent the problems of the passenger trade appear to have been seen by the Railway carrying committee as comparable to those of the carriage of passengers on the roads. For this reason, when investigating the possibility of contracting out the trade, it turned to Lacy, a leading Manchester coach proprietor.[42] From the point of view of the provision of accommodation, however, the experience of the coaching trade had only limited validity, for the road coach had a flexibility which enabled it to adapt to the existing pattern of hotels and inns. This the railway was less able to do. The carrying committee must also have been aware of the greater numbers it was likely to be called upon to deal with. If the average road coach

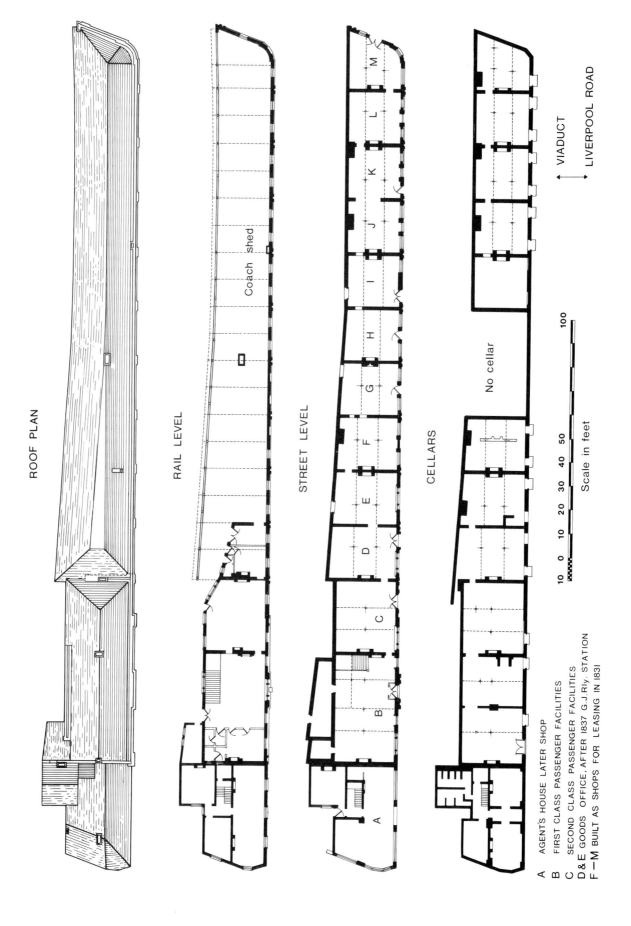

ROOF PLAN

RAIL LEVEL

Coach shed

STREET LEVEL

M

L

K

J

I

H

G

F

E

D

C

B

A

CELLARS

No cellar

VIADUCT

LIVERPOOL ROAD

10 0 10 20 30 40 50   100

Scale in feet

A   AGENT'S HOUSE LATER SHOP
B   FIRST CLASS PASSENGER FACILITIES
C   SECOND CLASS PASSENGER FACILITIES
D&E GOODS OFFICE, AFTER 1837 G.J.Rly. STATION
F—M BUILT AS SHOPS FOR LEASING IN 1831

The passenger station: ground plan as at June 1979.

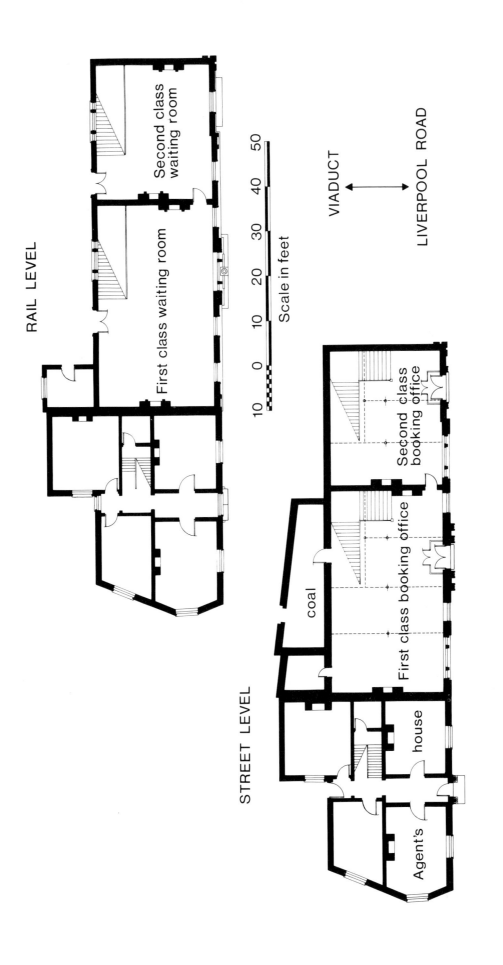

RAIL LEVEL

Second class waiting room

First class waiting room

Scale in feet

10   0   10   20   30   40   50

VIADUCT

LIVERPOOL ROAD

STREET LEVEL

coal

Second class booking office

First class booking office

house

Agent's

The passenger station and agent's house: reconstruction of ground plan in 1830.

carried between ten and fourteen people the Railway would need to multiply this figure by a factor of ten at least. The problem of up to two hundred people converging upon the train at one time had to be considered. Again the Railway Company found itself nearer in character to the canal trade than to other forms of land transport, but the lack of evidence that might give some impression of the form the canal companies' passenger accommodation took makes it difficult to assess the degree to which it influenced the station designs.

It cannot be said that the question of the design of the station bulked large in the Company's deliberations. Only the Crown Street depot is referred to up to mid-1830, and the Manchester station merited no comment. The planning and organisation of the building were apparently confined to the carrying committee, whose records have not survived. The obscurity which surrounds the building of the station extends further, for no specific provision occurs in the advertisements for tender which appeared in the *Manchester Guardian* of May 1830.[43] Only the warehouses are mentioned. That Bell-

(Below) this view of Liverpool Road and Water Street is the only one to show the bridge, the station and the warehouses. The station appears to be under construction. The detailing of the station is inaccurate, as are certain features of the bridge and warehouse. *(Right)* Liverpool Road Station: the first-class stairway.

house was responsible for the construction of the station building is implied by the *Manchester Courier* of 24 July 1830, which states that David Bellhouse had secured the contracts for the carriers' office adjacent to the station, the building of which was proceeding at that time.[44]

On 19 June 1830 the '. . . coach office . . . 80 feet long . . .' was about to be erected.[45] A month later it had reached second-storey level,[46] so it is safe to assume that by 15 September it was virtually complete. Even so, it played no part in the opening ceremony, the reception being confined to the warehouses. Scott Walker,[47] whose pamphlet is said to have been on sale at the opening of the line, gives this account of the building: '. . . opposite the warehouses on the other side of the railway is a spacious building with a Grecian front to the Liverpool Road. This will be the Station for the reception of passengers who will pass immediately through the building to and from the carriages . . .' A further brief allusion to the station appeared in 'Notes and Queries', derived from a diary kept by the father of a correspondent.[48] The entry for 27 October 1830 describes leaving Manchester by the ten o'clock train. The railroad was approached from the street by passing through the office, which contained a staircase to rail level.

Subsequently the station attracted little attention, and Wishaw, writing in 1839, devotes only a single sentence to it: '. . . The first and second class booking offices are on the level of Liverpool Road and the waiting rooms are over, at the same level as the railway and are approached by wide staircases from the ground floor . . .'[49]

Although the closure of the station to passengers in 1844 resulted in substantial alterations to the fabric of the building, sufficient remains to allow some evaluation of its original form to be made. The above accounts in summary give a building consisting of an 80 ft. street façade with four large rooms, two at each level, connected by staircases. The ground floor acted as the booking offices, and the upper floor as waiting rooms. The first and second-class passengers were segregated.

The original eastern gable of the building has been concealed by extensions and alterations, but its position is indicated by the hipped roof which remains, and the cornice which the eaves of the hip partly cover. The gable itself is unlikely to have carried any fenestration, for reasons which will be explained later. Internally, the principal division into first and second-class areas remains, the first-class area occupying rather more than half the ground plan with a length of 45 ft. and a width of 26 ft. The second-class rooms cover the remaining 30 ft. Partitions have divided the open spaces of the 1830s but

these can all be dismissed as subsequent,[50] the earliest being that located on the upper floor of the first-class section. Only the first-class staircase remains. The position of the second-class stairs can be located by the configuration of the floor beams, which follow the arrangement to be found in the first-class area, and by the boarding over of the stair void, the bridging joists of which do not correspond to the earlier floor layout. The doorways on to the viaduct are situated at the top of the respective stairs and, once again, only the first-class doorway is still intact. The second-class doorway is now bricked up, with a window occupying the upper half. Illumination for the stairs can be assumed to have been identical for the first and second class. The second-class window may well have been re-used when the corner of the building was canted at a later date. This latter development dictated the alteration to the second-class accommodation.

The rooms were heated by open fires, two for each of the first-class rooms, two for the second-class waiting room and one for the second-class booking office. The fireplace at the eastern end of the first-class waiting room is offset to accommodate the stairs. Its position in relation to the stairs is somewhat hazardous, but there is no indication that either the fireplace or the stairs are anything but contemporary. An extensive coal cellar was located adjacent to the railway arches, and a chute communicated with rail level. For the purpose of excluding draughts from the street doors a closed wooden lobby was constructed, and this remains in the first-class area. At rail level the former existence of a small out-building projecting northwards from the western extremity of the station building is denoted by a right-angled turn in the cornice moulding. The drawing shows this building conjecturally restored, using a site plan of 1867, and the form of the chamber located beneath, which aligns with the above-mentioned cornice detail.

The architectural treatment of the principal elevation has, for the purposes of the drawing, been derived from a photograph taken in 1903. As remarked by the observers quoted above, the order might be freely (perhaps rather too freely) described as 'Grecian Doric'. The superintendent's house was rather more academic in the use of classical orders, particularly in the doorcase. The building antedates the station and is known to have been in existence in 1825.[51] It was formerly the dwelling of John Rothwell, of the dyeworks partnership Rothwell Harrison.[52] The Railway Company acquired it along with the rest of the Rothwell Harrison property. It was occupied by Joseph Green, the Railway Company's agent for the Liverpool Road site from July 1830. The elevation of the

Agent's house   First class entrance   Second class entrance

Scale in feet

The passenger station and agent's house: reconstruction of Liverpool Road elevation in 1830.

Liverpool Road Station in 1905 *(above). (Right)* the first-class entrance. Its condition is that of 1830.

superintendent's house, with its exposed brick finish, contrasts with the station, which, although also of brick, is stuccoed with 'Roman Cement',[53] possibly Aspdin's hydraulic cement. The ground floor was treated with banded rustication separated from the first floor by a string course. The parapet was raised from a cornice to conceal the roofline. The first-class entrance was given due emphasis by paired pilaster strips and a heavy entablature topped by a curious baluster-cum-urn. The doorcase is echoed above by a five-light window with architraves and mullions repeating the design of the pilasters below. The window is headed by an entablature which also follows that of the doorcase in reduced form. In an attempt to achieve some symmetry the fenestration is paired on either side of the main entrance, and incised pilaster strips on the upper level seek to give an effect of unity. All this is completely destroyed by the second-class entrance and elevation, which are simply tacked on to the end of the first-class façade. In keeping with its status, it echoes the first-class entrance in a suitably diluted form. The rail elevation has no architectural pretensions. The brick walls were left exposed and the sole embellishment consists of a raised architrave around the doorways.

It has not proved possible to attribute the design of the building to any individual. As with the warehouse,

(*Above*) Liverpool Road Station façade, with the agent's house, the first-class entrance, the second-class entrance and the entrance to the carrier's office.

(*Below*) Liverpool Road Station from the railway side. The 1830 block occupies the centre; the covered shelter dates from 1831.

nowhere does there appear any reference to the party responsible. The Crown Street passenger station and Liverpool Road bear a sufficient similarity to each other to suggest that they emanate from the same hand. It is possible that they were a product of the Railway Company's own design office, but it may be more reasonable to suppose that the job was contracted out. The Liverpool architect and surveyor Thomas Haigh has already been discussed in connection with the warehouses, and the firm of Haigh Franklin continued to design new buildings for the Railway Company. In January 1831[54] they produced drawings for a new shed at Crosbie Street and six months later added another for the Bolton trade. They continued to be active throughout the 1830s. Unfortunately, from the point of view of identifying the authorship of the stations, they did not have a monopoly of the Railway Company's architectural works. The firm of Foster and Stewart was frequently consulted by the Railway Company, and Foster's connection with the Moorish arch at Edge Hill[55] is well known. In November 1830 Foster and Stewart provided the plans for the overall roof for Crown Street Station,[56] and five years later Foster was entrusted with the commission for the new Lime Street

Edge Hill Station, Liverpool, by Haigh and Franklin, 1835. The treatment of the elevation bears a strong resemblance to that of the earlier Liverpool Road Station, Manchester.

Bury print of Crown Street passenger station, Liverpool. The two-storey building incorporates the booking office and waiting rooms, whilst at the same time separating the road traffic from the railway. The overall roof dates from 1831.

Station at Liverpool, the most ambitious architectural project to be undertaken by the Company.[57] Haigh Franklin, however, were responsible for the Wavertree Lane station, built the year before.[58] It is also noteworthy that in 1834 Foster was stated by the chairman to have '. . . finished the design for the Moorish Arch . . . and had on other occasions rendered services . . . but . . . had received no remuneration for the same . . .'.[59]

It is particularly frustrating not to be able to give due credit for the design of these, the first two railway stations in the world, for not only are they intrinsically important but they acted as models for much of the first generation of stations. The essential features of the plan can best be seen at Crown Street, Liverpool, where the circumstances were uncomplicated by split levels. The linear plan oriented along the departure platform is clearly shown in the Ackermann print. The two-storey building contains offices and accommodation for the departing passengers and separates the railway from the courtyard into which the street traffic is allowed. The building thus combines the function of sheltering the waiting passengers with that of controlling access to the railway. This plan recurred wherever the Stephensons built railways. Even at Euston, where a superficial impression of an end-on layout prevailed by virtue of the Doric portico, 'all is sham'. The portico is irrelevant to the organisation of the station, for lurking behind is to be found the same layout of courtyard for road traffic, departure building and departure platform. The same is true of Curzon Street at Birmingham and the North Midland station at Leeds, the architect of which was Francis Thompson.[60] When simultaneous departures became common the design ceased to be serviceable and the end-on plan succeeded it.

The provision at Liverpool Road of office premises from which the carrying trade could be administered has all the appearance of being an afterthought. The station building had reached second-storey level when the *Manchester Courier*[61] announced that '. . . a building for the carrier's office has been contracted for by Mr. D. Bellhouse and the foundation is already laid . . .'. The building formed an eastward extension of the station range and perpetuated the architectural style of the station. The main entrance was almost identical in design to that of the second-class waiting rooms, but with reduced detail to conform with the hierarchical gradation of the façade. Two ground-floor rooms acted as parcels receiving point and office respectively. Communication with rail level seems to have been by way of the second-class booking

office staircase. The first-floor façade to Liverpool Road gives the impression of another level of rooms but in fact the wall is merely a screen, for behind is an open space.

The carrier's office was occupied by Joseph Green and his staff, but by 1834 he was expressing dissatisfaction with the arrangements because the isolation of the office from rail level hindered the efficient execution of his duties.[62] He advocated that new premises be built and that the existing office be converted to a dwelling for one of the Company's servants. The board took Green's point, and new offices were built adjacent to the down goods shed at the south-east corner of the site.[63]

· If the conversion of the carrier's office did take place, its existence as a dwelling was brief, for by 1837, at a cost of £720, it had become the station and office for the Grand Junction Railway.[64] It is this building that Wishaw referred to in 1839 as the Grand Junction's general booking office and waiting room above.[65] Wishaw implies that a further chamber had been built at rail level, although it is difficult to understand why the Liverpool and Manchester waiting rooms would not suffice. It may be that the upper room merely acted as an antechamber to the L. & M. rooms.

The remaining street frontage, is contemporary with the carrier's office. Scott Walker[66] seems to have been anticipating events when he wrote in 1830, '. . . besides the coach office there are in front several handsome shops . . .'. One shop at least was complete by July 1831, when William Vickers paid a rent of £35 to the Railway Company.[67] The Manchester rate book for 1832 lists Vic-

Liverpool Road: the shops, constructed in 1830–31.

The covered accommodation for twenty coaches, constructed about mid-1831.

kers's shop along with nine others, all of which were empty.[68] Vickers expanded his tenancy over the next ten years, and by 1836 one of his buildings had been converted into a beer shop, whilst the other two were offices.[69] Progressively the Company utilised an increasing number of these buildings for its own purposes.[70] In 1840 it had an engineer's office and a joiners' shop within them, but the beer shop remained, to achieve the status of a public house in July 1843, when the Railway applied for a licence for the premises. Only the street level was habitable, for, as with the coach office, the first-floor façade was simply a screen concealing a covered area for the accommodation of twenty railway coaches.

The passenger facilities which have been discussed so far were exclusively concerned with departures from Manchester. Arrival passengers were left in the hands of coach and omnibus operators, who ferried them into the town centre. The road transport awaited the trains on the north side of the Irwell Bridge, having approached the railway by means of a ramp up from Water Street.[71] Until October 1831 the standing area was unpaved.[72] In July 1833 a minor concession was made to arrival passengers when the landing stage on the bridge was roofed over by an open shed, supported upon cast-iron columns.[73] Although the directors were increasingly aware of the need to improve the arrival accommodation, their actions were restrained by uncertainty over the impact that the London and Birmingham trade might have when the Grand Junction Railway was completed.[74] The board had also to consider the possibility of the railway penetrating farther into Manchester.[75]

In mid-1835 plans for a new arrival station to occupy the site of the Rothwell Harrison dyeworks had been submitted to the board,[76] but two years elapsed before the project was embarked upon. In August 1836 tenders had been invited for the construction of '. . . a range of warehouses, sheds, offices and appurtenances with approach road to be supported principally on arches from Water Street to the Irwell Bridge for the purpose of an arrival station . . .',[77] but the cost of the project seems to have deterred the board from proceeding. The contract was re-advertised in May 1837[78] and let the following month to William and Henry Southern for £7,999.[79] To designs by Haigh Franklin, a range of buildings was to be constructed on the west side of Water Street, the contract to include an approach road on arches with a covered colonnade beneath which were stables. The new station was opened in December 1837.[80] The main block was of two storeys from rail level, 156 ft. long and 51 ft. deep. A canopy extended from the front of the building to the rails, supported at 13 ft. intervals by cast-iron columns. At the western end of the station a carriage dock was built for off-loading road vehicles from the trains. Access to Water Street was by means of a ramp down from the railway to the rear of the building.[81]

Between 1850 and 1867 the London and North Western Railway, into which the Liverpool and Manchester had by now been subsumed, set about redeveloping the Liverpool Road site. The boundary was extended eastwards to New Street and the transit shed of 1831 demolished to make way for an enlarged building of generally similar design completed about 1855. In the mid-1860s warehouses 2 and 3 were removed to make way for an additional viaduct consisting of cast-iron columns and fabricated wrought-iron beams running parallel to the present Grape Street. The warehouse facilities were enlarged by the construction of two additional buildings to serve the needs of the London and North Western and the Great Western Railway, which had obtained running powers into the site. These buildings were known respectively as the London and North Western bonded warehouse and the Great Western warehouse. At the same time the arrival station was demolished to make way for improved access to the newly developed site.

Although the Liverpool and Manchester Railway has always been a heavily used line, a high proportion of the original civil engineering features remain in use. The continued existence of so many of the brick and masonry arches is unsurprising, for by their nature such structures are relatively understressed. That the station building and the goods warehouse at Liverpool Road should still survive is more remarkable. Very few other early station buildings remain and, as far as is known, nothing comparable to the warehouse still stands. Manchester thus possesses bridges, a station and a warehouse of the utmost importance in the history of railway engineering and architecture. Their restoration is to be applauded, and their assured future as the home of the North Western Museum of Science and Industry is both welcome and apt.

Notes

[1] Tomlinson, *The North Eastern Railway*, pp. 116 ff.

[2] Minutes of the Board of Directors, 26 May 1828.

[3] *Ibid.*, 30 June 1828.

[4] *Ibid.*, 29 June 1829.

[5] *Ibid.*, 14 September 1829.

[6] *Ibid.*, 21 September 1829.

[7] *Ibid.*, 21 November 1829.

[8] *Ibid.*, 21 November 1829.

[9] *Ibid.*, 11 January 1830.

[10] *Ibid.*, 21 November 1829.

[11] Carlson, *The Liverpool and Manchester Railway Project*, p. 47.

[12] Information extracted from local directories by the staff of the Liverpool Public Library, to whom my thanks are due.

[13] This building was occupying its present site by 1826, but it is believed to have been moved from a previous site in Yorkshire.

[14] V. I. Tomlinson, 'Early Warehouses on Manchester Waterways', *Transactions of the Lancashire and Cheshire Antiquarian Society*, 1961.

[15] *Ibid.*

[16] Diaries and MS Autobiography of Thomas L. Gooch.

[17] Minutes of the Board of Directors, 17 May 1830.

[18] Directories for the Liverpool area, 1807 to 1832.

[19] Minutes of the Board of Directors, 14 March 1831.

[20] *Report of the Annual General Meeting of the Liverpool and Manchester Railway Company*, March 1830. This was published in 1831, after the railway had opened. Bound copies in the City of Manchester Reference Library, Local History section.

[21] *Manchester Guardian*, 3 April 1830.

[22] Minutes of the Board of Directors, 26 November 1829.

[23] *Ibid.*, 19 April 1830.

[24] *Ibid.*, 26 April 1830.

[25] Mortgage document in the City of Manchester Archives Department, 19/40/2.

[26] *Manchester Chronicle*, 7 February 1824.

[27] Manchester Poor Rate Book, 1826, vol. 94, District 10, City of Manchester Archives Department.

[28] Minutes of the Board of Directors, 17 May 1830.

[29] *Manchester Guardian*, 24 July 1830.

[30] *Ibid.*

[31] Minutes of the Board of Directors, 31 January 1831.

[32] *Ibid.*, 1 November 1830, 2 May 1831.

[33] *Manchester Guardian*, 4 September 1834.

[34] Minutes of the Board of Directors, 7 March 1831.

[35] *Ibid.*, 6 June 1831.

[36] Wishaw, *The Railways of Great Britain and Ireland*, p. 200.

[37] Minutes of the Board of Directors, 26 February 1838.

[38] Incorporated in 1846 by amalgamation of the London and Birmingham, Grand Junction, Manchester and Birmingham, and other lines, including the Liverpool and Manchester.

[39] Hadfield and Biddle, *The Canals of North West England*, p. 35.

[40] C. F. Dendy Marshall, *A History of British Railways down to the Year 1830*, Oxford University Press, 1938, pp. 81 ff.

[41] Tomlinson, *The North Eastern Railway*, pp. 116 ff.

[42] Minutes of the Board of Directors, 14 September 1829.

[43] *Manchester Guardian*, 3 May 1830.

[44] *Manchester Courier*, 24 July 1830.

[45] *Wheeler's Manchester Chronicle*, 19 June 1830.

[46] *Manchester Courier*, 24 July 1830.

[47] J. Scott Walker, *An Accurate Description of the Liverpool and Manchester Railway*, 1830, rpr. Lancashire and Cheshire Anti-

quarian Society, 1968, p. 43.

[48] Quoted in Richard Pike, *The Romance of the Liverpool and Manchester Railway.*

[49] Wishaw, *The Railways of Great Britain and Ireland*, p. 199.

[50] Dating by cornice mouldings and fabric.

[51] Committee on the Liverpool and Manchester Railroad, *Proceedings of the Committee of the House of Commons on the Liverpool and Manchester Railroad Bill*, 1825, map.

[52] Manchester Poor Rate Book, vol. 94, District 10, 1826, Manchester Public Library Archives Department.

[53] *Wheeler's Manchester Chronicle*, 19 June 1830.

[54] Minutes of the Board of Directors, 14 March 1831.

[55] *Ibid.*, 18 August 1828. Foster was requested to provide a design for the principal frontage to the engine houses, the plans for which had been prepared by Stephenson.

[56] *Ibid.*, 1 November 1830.

[57] *Ibid.*, 20 April 1835.

[58] *Ibid.*, 29 December 1834.

[59] *Ibid.*, 1 August 1834.

[60] Wishaw, *The Railways of Great Britain and Ireland*; see also Ordnance Survey 60 in. plans published in the early 1850s for Leeds, Birmingham and London.

[61] *Manchester Courier*, 24 July 1831.

[62] Minutes of the Board of Directors, 9 June 1834.

[63] *Ibid.*, 22 September 1834.

[64] *Ibid.*, 13 February 1837.

[65] Wishaw, *The Railways of Great Britain and Ireland*, p. 199.

[66] Scott Walker, *An Accurate Description . . .*, p. 44.

[67] Minutes of the meetings of the Committee of Management, 27 July 1831.

[68] Manchester Poor Rate Book, vol. 107, District 10, 1832.

[69] *Ibid.*, vol. 118, District 10, 1836.

[70] *Ibid.*, vol. 130, District 10, 1840.

[71] Wishaw, *The Railways of Great Britain and Ireland*, p. 199.

[72] Minutes of the Committee of Management, 10 October 1831.

[73] *Ibid.*, 1 July 1833.

[74] *Ibid.*, 9 March 1835.

[75] *Ibid.*, 15 June 1835.

[76] *Ibid.*, 8 June 1835.

[77] *Manchester Guardian*, 20 August 1836.

[78] Minutes of the Committee of Management, 17 May 1837.

[79] Minutes of the Board of Directors, 12 June 1837 and 19 February 1838.

[80] *Ibid.*, 14 December 1837.

[81] Wishaw, *The Railways of Great Britain and Ireland*, p. 199.

Index